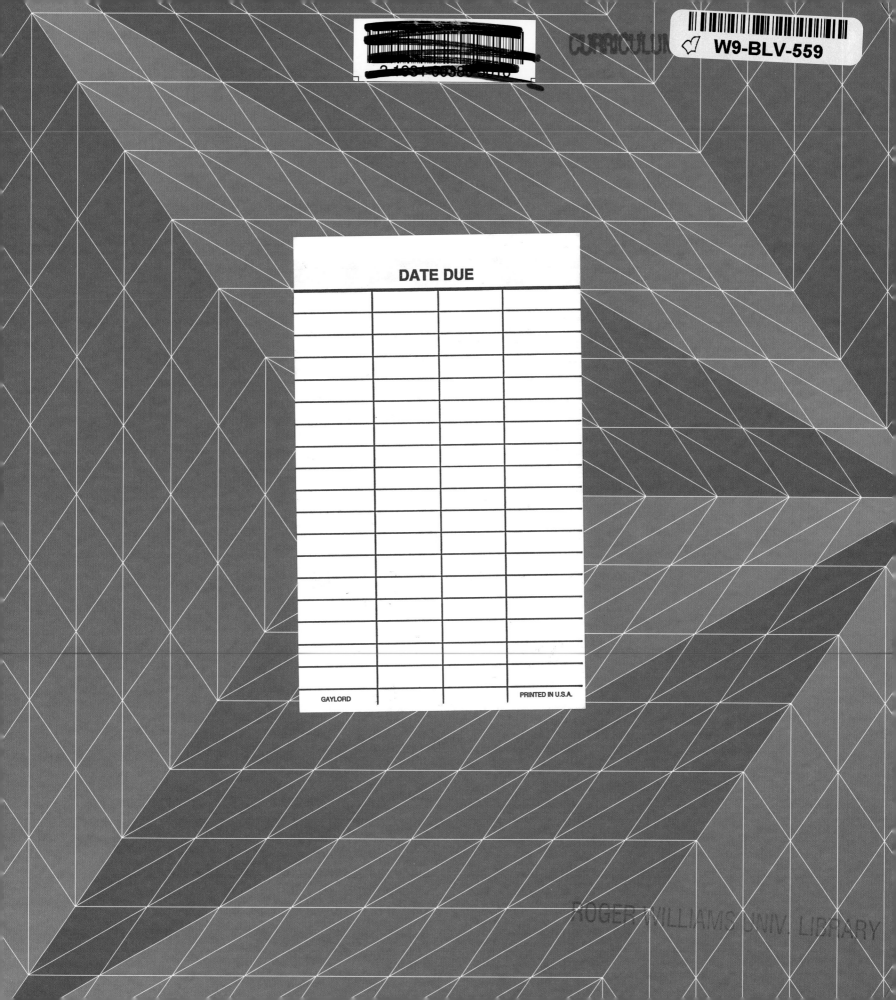

Sharks

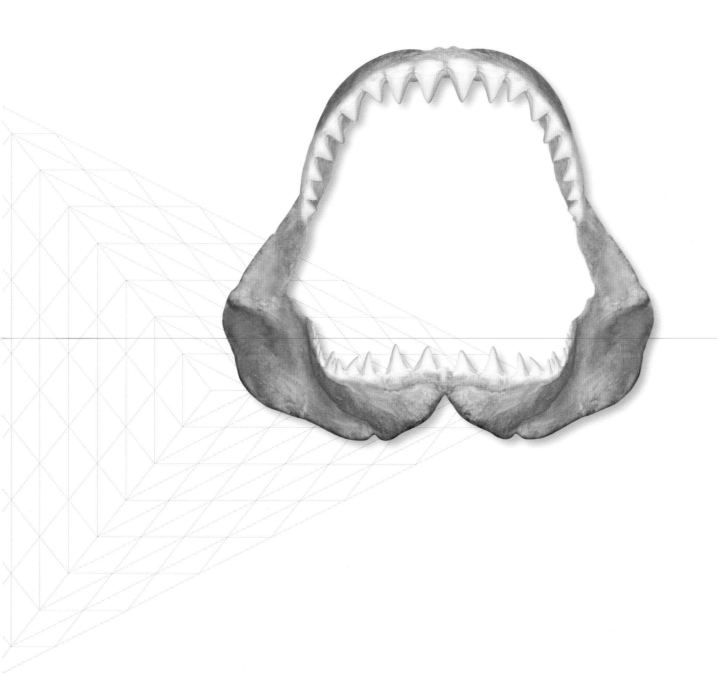

SIMON & SCHUSTER BOOKS FOR YOUNG READERS
An imprint of Simon & Schuster Children's Publishing Division
1230 Avenue of the Americas, New York, New York 10020

Conceived and produced by Weldon Owen Pty Ltd
59-61 Victoria Street, McMahons Point
Sydney, NSW 2060, Australia

WELDON OWEN GROUP
Chairman John Owen

WELDON OWEN PTY LTD
Chief Executive Officer Sheena Coupe
Creative Director Sue Burk
Concept Development John Bull, The Book Design Company
Publishing Coordinator Mike Crowton
Senior Vice President, International Sales Stuart Laurence
Vice President, Sales and New Business Development Amy Kaneko
Vice President, Sales: Asia and Latin America Dawn Low
Administrator, International Sales Kristine Ravn

Project Editor Jenni Bruce
Designer Helen Woodward, Flow Design & Communications
Cover Designers Gaye Allen, Kelly Booth, Brandi Valenza
Design Assistant Sarah Norton
Art Manager Trucie Henderson
Illustrators The Art Agency (Thomas Bayley, Robin Carter, Barry Croucher,
Rob Davis, Gary Hanna, Terry Pastor, Mick Posen), Christer Eriksson

Color reproduction by Chroma Graphics (Overseas) Pte Ltd
Printed by SNP Leefung Printers Ltd
Manufactured in China

A WELDON OWEN PRODUCTION

SIMON & SCHUSTER BOOKS FOR YOUNG READERS is a trademark of Simon & Schuster, Inc.
The text for this book is set in Meta and Rotis Serif.
10 9 8 7 6 5 4 3 2 1
Cataloging-in-publication data for this book is available from the Library of Congress.
ISBN-13: 978-1-4169-3867-5
ISBN-10: 1-4169-3867-2

Sharks

Beverly McMillan and John A. Musick

Simon & Schuster Books for Young Readers
New York London Toronto Sydney

Contents

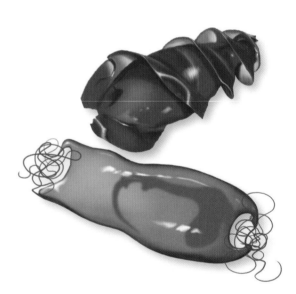

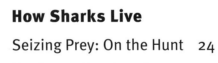

 *focus*

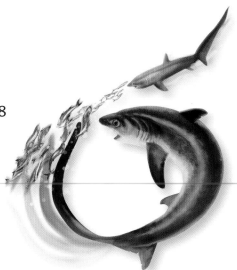

introducing

What Is
A Shark?

Inside and out, a shark is like no other fish in the sea. For millions of years sharks have ruled as fast-swimming predators—all without a single bone in their body. Instead, a shark has a skeleton of cartilage that supports its powerful muscles and fins, forms its amazing toothy jaws, and shields its hunter's brain. Sharks are also the only fish with scales that resemble tiny, overlapping teeth. Most baby fish are nearly defenseless, but shark pups are keen hunters from the moment they are born. And while other fish die after a few years, many sharks have a long natural life span. They may cruise the deep for 20, 30, 40 years or more.

SHARK SHAPES

From basking sharks as long as a bus to species that would fit in a coat pocket, sharks come in all sizes and shapes. Most have a tapered, hydrodynamic body and fins that help them glide smoothly through the water. Nearly all species have five gill slits on each side of the head and a pointed snout with the mouth behind the tip.

Angel shark With its flattened body, an angel shark looks almost like a ray.

Bronze whaler Like most sharks, the bronze whaler has a streamlined shape.

Frilled shark This sinewy shark is one of the few sharks with six pairs of gill slits.

Basking shark Huge baskers often loll at the surface, feeding on tiny plankton.

Head protection *Like the bony skull of a human, a shark's skull-like cartilage cranium protects the brain, eyes, and other vital soft body parts in a shark's head. Blood vessels and nerves snake through openings in the cartilage.*

See-through shark

This X-ray view reveals the framework of a typical shark and highlights some of the characteristics that have made sharks such successful ocean predators—a mouthful of impressive teeth, powerful jaws that can open wide to engulf prey, and a skeleton of strong, flexible cartilage.

Fins up!
All sharks have one or two dorsal fins. The first dorsal fin is often much larger. Fast swimmers have a small second dorsal fin, making their body more streamlined.

Whale shark This enormous shark's dorsal fin can be more than 5 feet (1.5 m) tall.

Zebra shark The low and long dorsal fins of this slow shark are spotted like the rest of its body.

Tail power
A shark's tail helps push its body forward as it swims. Fast-swimming species have a stiff crescent-shaped tail that provides plenty of power. More sluggish sharks have a longer, snaky tail.

Porbeagle One of the speediest sharks, the porbeagle has a crescent-shaped tail.

Thresher shark A thresher uses its extra-long tail to stun prey fish.

Chain catshark This slow-swimming catshark has a long, slender tail.

Oceanic whitetip A large, angled tail propels this shark through open ocean.

Horn shark These sharks are named for sharp spines in front of their dorsal fins.

Blacktip reef shark This shark gets its name from its coal-black fin markings.

Great white This broad first dorsal fin dwarfs a tiny second dorsal fin.

Swimming Machines

For many sharks, life is a never-ending swim. Night and day, such sharks must stay on the move, forcing water over their gills to deliver oxygen into their bloodstream. If the shark stops to rest, it will suffocate and die. All parts of a shark contribute to their superb hydrodynamic design. A sleek shape and an unusual skin of tiny toothlike scales help the shark to glide smoothly through the seas. A strong but rubbery cartilage skeleton allows flexible movements of the body. Even the muscles are fine-tuned: Some muscles work steadily during long-distance cruising, while others power swift attacks on prey.

Swimming not required
Not all sharks need to keep swimming to breathe. As this epaulette shark rests on the bottom, its muscles pump seawater in through openings called spiracles, over the gills, and out again.

Cartilage skeleton
From its cranium to the tip of its tail, a shark's skeleton is made of flexible cartilage. Cartilage is lighter than bone, so a shark needs less energy to stay aloft in the water.

Red and white *A shortfin mako's white outer muscles contract strongly for a short time to provide bursts of speed. When the shark is just steadily cruising, strips of crimson-red muscle along its sides do most of the work.*

Growth rings *As a shark grows, rings of cartilage form in the vertebrae of its spine. Like the growth rings of a tree, the rings in a shark's vertebrae can be counted to provide an estimate of its age.*

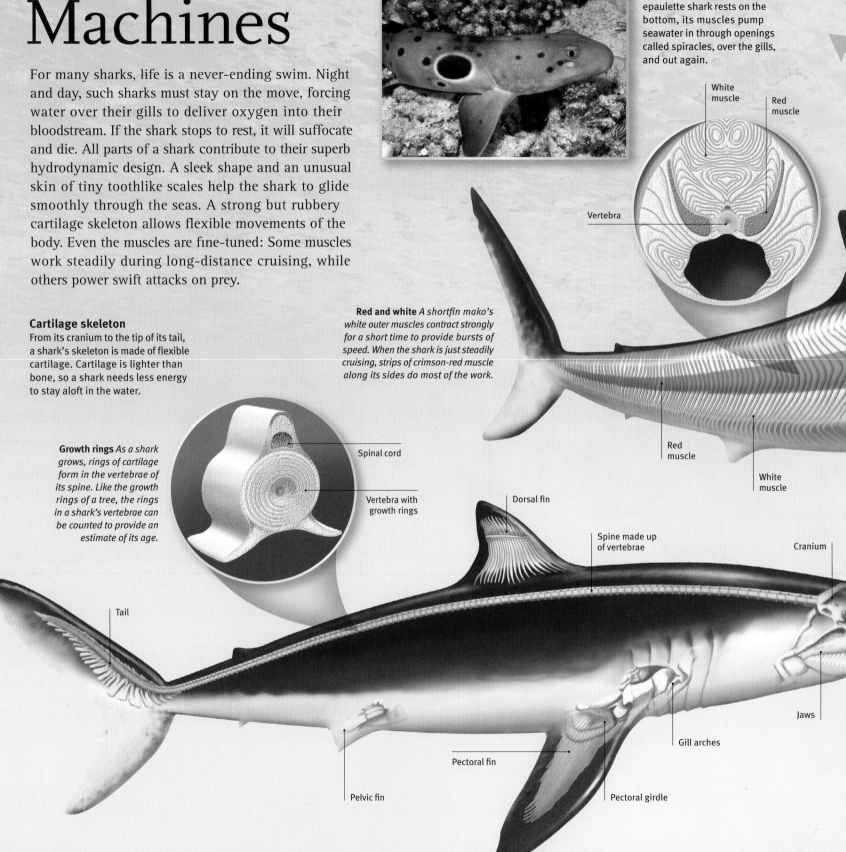

White muscle

Red muscle

Vertebra

Red muscle

White muscle

Spinal cord

Vertebra with growth rings

Dorsal fin

Spine made up of vertebrae

Cranium

Tail

Jaws

Gill arches

Pectoral fin

Pectoral girdle

Pelvic fin

Gravity

Thrust
from tail

Buoyancy

Lift from
tail in motion

Drag

Defying gravity *Buoyancy and lift from a shark's liver, tail, pectoral fins, and forebody help offset the force of gravity, which pulls it downward in the water. The constantly beating tail also provides thrust to overcome the slowing effects of drag.*

Lift from
pectoral fins
and forebody

Tough, scaly skin

Tough scales called dermal denticles blanket a shark's body. Each shark species has a distinctive denticle shape, often with ridges and grooves. Scientists have found that dermal denticles reduce friction by directing the flow of water.

Enamel

Dentine

Epidermis

Dermis

Pulp cavity

Dermal
denticles

Muscle power

Zigzag blocks of muscle work together to power a shark's lifelong swim. Swimming muscles make up as much as 65 percent of the shark's body weight.

High seas speedster

The shortfin mako has the body of an ocean athlete. It is shaped like a torpedo and has a crescent-shaped tail. Both these features help overcome drag as the shark speeds through the water. This species also has the muscle power to rocket from the water like a missile. Makos have astonished fishermen by leaping into their boats.

Toothy scale *A dermal denticle resembles a tooth. As small as a pinhead and as strong as steel, each denticle has an enamel tip, a layer of bony tissue known as dentine, and a cavity full of soft pulp, along with nerves and blood vessels. Sharks are the only fish that have dermal denticles.*

How a shark swims

Side-to-side movements of a shark's body drive it through the water. The wavy body motion is more extreme when the shark is accelerating and smooths out while it is cruising.

1. When muscles along one side of the shark's spine contract, its body bends.

2. Strong thrust from the lashing tail pushes the shark's body forward.

3. As muscles on the other side of the spine contract, the shark continues to swim.

A Shark's
Insides

Every moment of a shark's life, its internal organs are working like the parts of a living engine. Sharks have many of the same organs that people do, such as a brain, a stretchy stomach, kidneys, and a blood-pumping heart. But a shark's insides are also adapted to undersea life. The gills move oxygen from seawater into the shark's blood and get rid of the waste carbon dioxide. A liver packed with oil makes a shark more buoyant so that it needs less energy to stay afloat and swim. In some sharks special networks of blood vessels warm the brain, eyes, and swimming muscles—ensuring that the shark remains alert and ready to pursue its active life in the sea.

How smart are sharks?
Sharks can learn from experience, but they generally operate on instinct. One clue to animal intelligence is the weight of an animal's brain compared to the rest of its body. Another indicator is the complexity of the brain's structure.

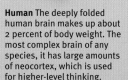

Human The deeply folded human brain makes up about 2 percent of body weight. The most complex brain of any species, it has large amounts of neocortex, which is used for higher-level thinking.

Dolphin A dolphin's brain usually weighs less than 1 percent of its body weight. Even so, dolphins learn fast and seem highly intelligent compared to seals and other marine mammals.

Inside a salmon shark
Fast-swimming salmon sharks live in the North Pacific Ocean, where salmon are their favorite food. Even in the icy water, four "wonderful nets" of blood vessels, each called a rete mirabile, help keep the salmon shark's blood around 78°F (26°C)—warmer than an average room. This salmon shark is a female, and her reproductive organs include two uteri, where pups grow.

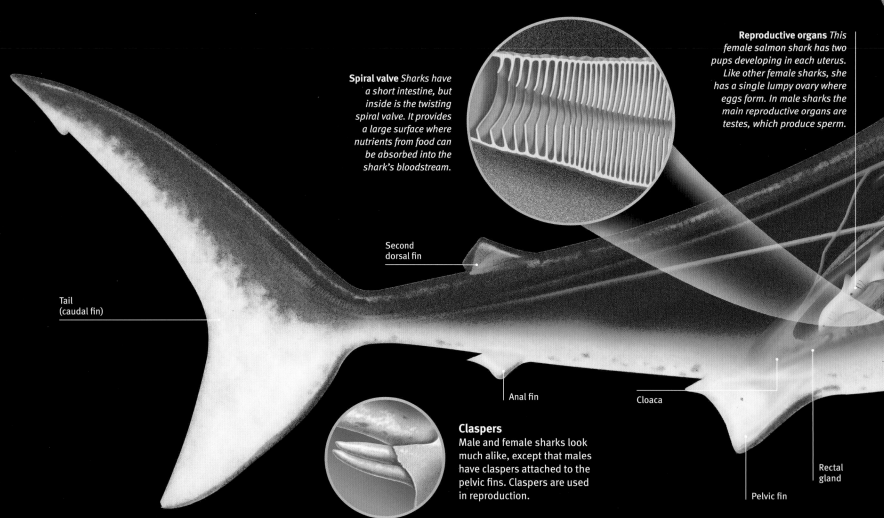

Spiral valve *Sharks have a short intestine, but inside is the twisting spiral valve. It provides a large surface where nutrients from food can be absorbed into the shark's bloodstream.*

Reproductive organs *This female salmon shark has two pups developing in each uterus. Like other female sharks, she has a single lumpy ovary where eggs form. In male sharks the main reproductive organs are testes, which produce sperm.*

Second dorsal fin

Tail (caudal fin)

Anal fin

Cloaca

Claspers
Male and female sharks look much alike, except that males have claspers attached to the pelvic fins. Claspers are used in reproduction.

Rectal gland

Pelvic fin

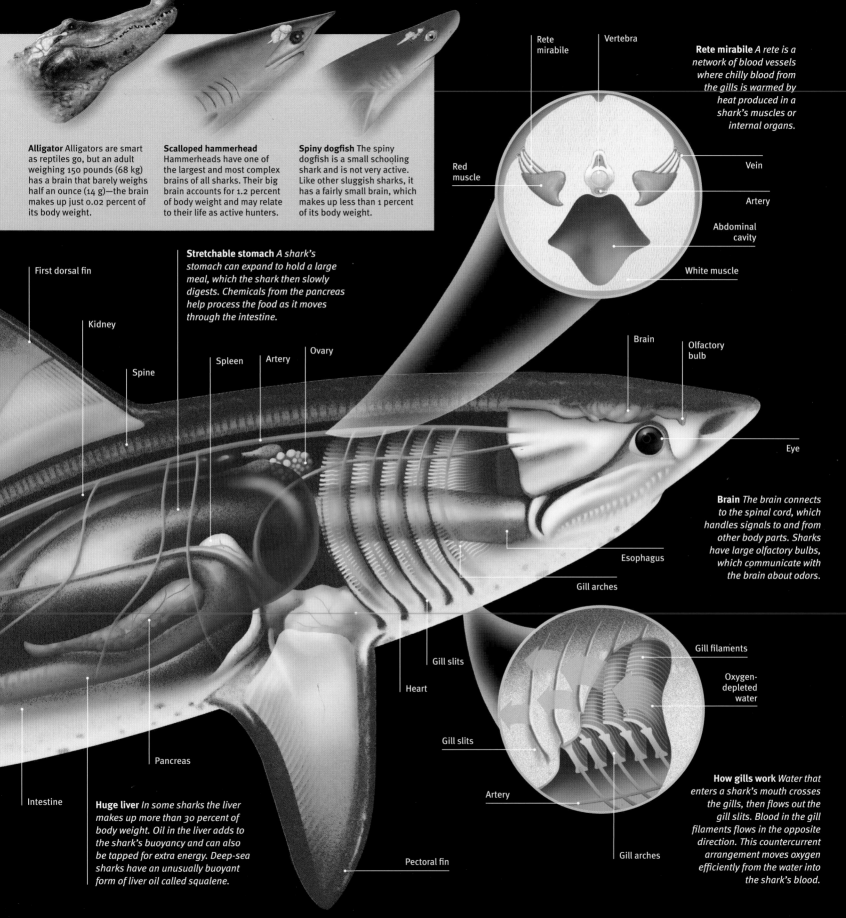

Alligator Alligators are smart as reptiles go, but an adult weighing 150 pounds (68 kg) has a brain that barely weighs half an ounce (14 g)—the brain makes up just 0.02 percent of its body weight.

Scalloped hammerhead Hammerheads have one of the largest and most complex brains of all sharks. Their big brain accounts for 1.2 percent of body weight and may relate to their life as active hunters.

Spiny dogfish The spiny dogfish is a small schooling shark and is not very active. Like other sluggish sharks, it has a fairly small brain, which makes up less than 1 percent of its body weight.

Rete mirabile *A rete is a network of blood vessels where chilly blood from the gills is warmed by heat produced in a shark's muscles or internal organs.*

Rete mirabile

Vertebra

Red muscle

Vein

Artery

Abdominal cavity

White muscle

Stretchable stomach *A shark's stomach can expand to hold a large meal, which the shark then slowly digests. Chemicals from the pancreas help process the food as it moves through the intestine.*

First dorsal fin

Kidney

Spine

Spleen

Artery

Ovary

Brain

Olfactory bulb

Eye

Brain *The brain connects to the spinal cord, which handles signals to and from other body parts. Sharks have large olfactory bulbs, which communicate with the brain about odors.*

Esophagus

Gill arches

Gill slits

Heart

Gill filaments

Oxygen-depleted water

Gill slits

Artery

Gill arches

How gills work *Water that enters a shark's mouth crosses the gills, then flows out the gill slits. Blood in the gill filaments flows in the opposite direction. This countercurrent arrangement moves oxygen efficiently from the water into the shark's blood.*

Intestine

Pancreas

Huge liver *In some sharks the liver makes up more than 30 percent of body weight. Oil in the liver adds to the shark's buoyancy and can also be tapped for extra energy. Deep-sea sharks have an unusually buoyant form of liver oil called squalene.*

Pectoral fin

Sensory
Superstars

In the depths or shallows, sharks hunt prey with pinpoint accuracy thanks to their champion senses. Hearing is a shark's long-distance prey detector—its ears are hidden inside its head and can pick up the sound of a thrashing fish as far as 1,650 feet (500 m) away. Sharks also rely on an astounding sense of smell. Put a lemon shark in a large swimming pool and it will detect the scent of only a few drops of blood. In clear ocean water, a shark following a sound or scent trail may see its prey some 80 feet (25 m) away. After making a stealthy approach, the shark will rely on its keen electric sense to guide its powerful bite for the crucial last inches.

Following the sensory clues

Sound is this silky shark's first clue that a feast of bluefin tuna may be near. Swimming toward the sound, the next major clue may be a scent such as blood, or vibrations in the water caused by the prey's movements. Electricity produced by the tuna's heart or muscles is like a beacon that allows the shark to zero in on its target in the final instants before the kill.

4 Pressure detection *The fluid-filled canals in a shark's lateral line system operate like a string of motion sensors. They can detect pressure changes caused by even slight vibrations in the water.*

Lateral line

Skin pore

Nerve   Mucus-filled canal

1 Hearing *Two tiny pores on the top of a shark's head open to channels leading to its inner ears, which detect sound waves. Semicircular canals sense signals about the shark's body movements and help to regulate its balance.*

2 Smell *Inside a shark's nostrils are folds called lamellae. They are sprinkled with receptors that can detect microscopic amounts of proteins from the prey's blood or other body fluids.*

Skin

Semicircular canals

Inner ear

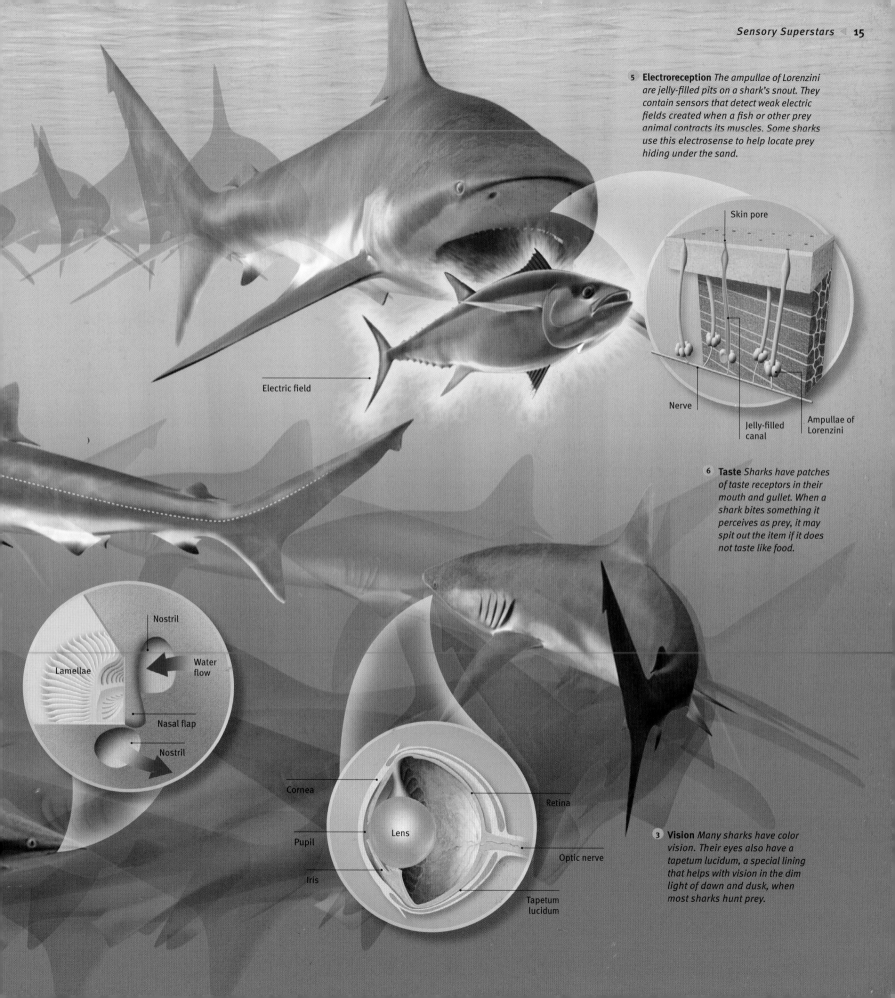

5 **Electroreception** *The ampullae of Lorenzini are jelly-filled pits on a shark's snout. They contain sensors that detect weak electric fields created when a fish or other prey animal contracts its muscles. Some sharks use this electrosense to help locate prey hiding under the sand.*

Skin pore

Nerve

Jelly-filled canal

Ampullae of Lorenzini

6 **Taste** *Sharks have patches of taste receptors in their mouth and gullet. When a shark bites something it perceives as prey, it may spit out the item if it does not taste like food.*

Electric field

Nostril

Water flow

Lamellae

Nasal flap

Nostril

Cornea

Pupil

Iris

Lens

Retina

Optic nerve

Tapetum lucidum

3 **Vision** *Many sharks have color vision. Their eyes also have a tapetum lucidum, a special lining that helps with vision in the dim light of dawn and dusk, when most sharks hunt prey.*

A Mouthful of
Teeth

A shark's awesome teeth are tailor-made for capturing its meals. Even big, powerful prey like whales and seals are no match for a great white shark's huge triangular teeth. The pointed lower teeth of a Caribbean reef shark are excellent tools for spearing fleeing fish. On the other hand, sharks that hunt along the seafloor for crabs and clams have sturdy, tilelike teeth that make quick work of crushing hard shells. Losing or breaking a tooth is no problem for a shark—new teeth are always growing and replacing the old. Fossil beds contain countless millions of shark teeth, and ocean waves bring millions more ashore.

Great teeth for the great white

Its mouth gaping wide, a great white bares the shark world's largest and most fearsome teeth. When the shark targets prey, it lunges up from below. As its teeth sink into the prey's flesh, the great white shakes its head from side to side so its jaws cut like massive saw blades. For most prey, capture by a great white is certain death.

Jagged edge
Inside a great white's vast mouth are about 50 deadly teeth. Broad, thick, and serrated like steak knives, the teeth are ideal tools for slicing up prey.

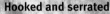

Shell crushers
The Port Jackson shark has small, pointed front teeth for holding prey such as sea urchins and crabs, while the broad, flat back teeth can crush the prey's shell. A full upper jaw is shown here.

Hooked and serrated
With its small, hooked upper teeth and large, serrated lower teeth, the kitefin shark can catch whole fish and ink-squirting squid and also bite lumps of blubber from whales.

Spearing teeth
The pale goblin shark uses the electrosensory organs of its snout to detect octopuses, squid, shrimps, and fish, and then spears the prey with its fine, needle-like front teeth.

Can-opener jaws
The voracious tiger shark may swallow an unsuspecting seabird whole. With its rounded, sawlike teeth, this shark can even tackle sea turtles. If the teeth were more pointed, they would probably break on a turtle's shell.

Eyes out of the way *When a great white attacks, its eyes roll backward so they are shielded from thrashing prey. Some other shark species have a special membrane that protects the eyes.*

Snout up *As a shark strikes, its snout rises and the jaws shoot forward. The way is now clear for the shark's exposed teeth to pierce its victim.*

Sawlike teeth *This adult great white's upper teeth are broad, thick triangles, while its lower teeth are a bit narrower. A young great white has spearlike lower teeth to catch its fish prey.*

Gill arches *Active sharks like the great white have five curved cartilage gill arches on either side of the head. These arches support the shark's gills, which take in oxygen from seawater.*

New teeth *Rows of smaller teeth are always developing behind the full-grown teeth in a shark's jaws. Every so often a new row moves forward like a toothy conveyor belt, and the old teeth fall out.*

Incredible Jaws
The Big Bite

The fierce bite of a shark combines lightning speed with steely strength. Whether a shark is hunting a small fish to swallow whole or large prey that it will rip to pieces, its unusual jaws give it a keen competitive edge. Usually set back under a shark's head, the jaws are protrusible—powerful muscles can push them up and outward. In the split second before a shark attacks, its jaws thrust forward and open wide, razor-sharp teeth ready to grasp, pierce, or slice into the prey's body. The chance of escape is slim: species such as the tiger shark bite down with more than 20 tons (18t) of crushing force.

3 **Out and up** *Now the sand tiger's jaws are open wide. The upper jaw juts out of the mouth while the backward-curving lower teeth become fully exposed—ready to pierce and hold the little sandbar shark.*

2 **Sliding jaw** *Next the shark's snout tilts up, the upper jaw starts to slide forward, and the lower jaw drops down. The shark's mouth is beginning to open.*

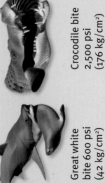

JAWS OF STEEL

All bites are not alike. Human jaws have a fairly strong bite, and dog jaws are stronger still. Even the great white shark's powerful jaws are no match for the bone-crushing bite of a crocodile. Researchers have measured bite force in pounds per square inch (psi), or kilograms per square centimeter (kg/cm²), but there is no way of knowing for sure whether the test animal is biting at maximum strength.

Rottweiler bite
328 psi
(23 kg/cm²)

Crocodile bite
2,500 psi
(176 kg/cm²)

Human bite
120 psi
(8 kg/cm²)

Great white
bite 600 psi
(42 kg/cm²)

Biting action

When a hungry sand tiger shark overtakes a baby sandbar shark, it captures its meal in a flash. Using specialized video cameras and other high-tech tools, scientists discovered that a shark's jaws move in an amazing rapid-fire sequence of steps that takes less than a single second from start to finish.

Rolling eye *Before the sand tiger bites, its eye is exposed. Just as the shark closes in on its prey, the eye rolls backward into its head.*

Tooth replacement
Because rows of new teeth are constantly moving up to the front of a shark's jaws, a shark can afford to lose or damage teeth when it is trying to catch prey. Some sharks lose tens of thousands of teeth during their life.

① **Before the bite** *A shark's jaws are built of pieces of cartilage that interlock below the cranium. Muscles and ligaments hold the pieces loosely in place. As a bite starts, the jaws are relaxed and slightly agape.*

How jaws measure up

Shark jaws are measured by gape—the width, corner to corner, and the height of the jaw opening. Among sharks, only the whale shark and basking shark have a gape larger than that of the great white. The jaws here are shown to scale beside a 10-year-old girl.

Sand tiger shark
Width 9 in (23 cm)
Height 7 in (18 cm)

Blacktip shark
Width 6 in (15 cm)
Height 5 in (13 cm)

Gray smoothhound shark
Width 2 in (5 cm)
Height 1.5 in (4 cm)

10-year-old girl
Height 54 in (137 cm)

Great white shark
Width 28 in (71 cm)
Height 27.5 in (70 cm)

Amazing speed

A lemon shark's jaws can grab its prey in less than two-tenths of a second. That is about twice as fast as you can blink, and four times faster than a single beat of your heart.

Human heartbeat
0.8 second

Human eye-blink
0.3–0.4 second

Lemon shark bite
0.2 second

▲ 1 second ▼

Sharks Through
The Ages

Among superpredators, sharks hold the world record for staying power—they have been hunting the seas for more than 400 million years. Long before fierce dinosaurs roamed Earth, the oceans were home to ancestors of modern sharks. Fossils reveal the mystery of these shark pioneers, some with weird curling whorls of teeth, giant bony spines, or other strange body parts. Over the ages many ancient shark relatives went extinct and new ones evolved. The march of time slowly shaped sharks into today's streamlined swimmers, with protrusible jaws, keen senses, and other features that make them awesome ocean predators.

SHARK FOSSILS

Hard and bony shark teeth make good fossils because they do not decay when they are buried in mud or sand. Much rarer are fossils of the soft cartilage skeleton. Scientists often must use bits and pieces to guess what a shark looked like.

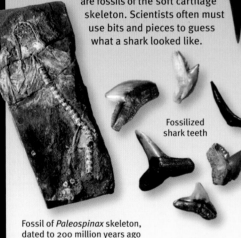

Fossilized shark teeth

Fossil of *Paleospinax* skeleton, dated to 200 million years ago

*mya = million years ago

Devonian shark: 370 mya*
Cladoselache *was one of the early sharks known as cladodonts. Its teeth had more than one spiky cusp, and its mouth was at the tip of its snout. With a crescent-shaped tail, it was probably a fast open-water swimmer.*

Carboniferous shark: 320 mya *Odd-looking* Stethacanthus *males had a bizarre "scrub brush" on their first dorsal fin and a matching set of bristles atop their head. These strange parts may have been used during mating.*

CAMBRIAN PERIOD	ORDOVICIAN PERIOD	SILURIAN PERIOD	DEVONIAN PERIOD	CARBONIFEROUS PERIOD
550 mya Animals with shells and jawless fish (first vertebrates) evolve	**505 mya** Jawless fish diversify and jawed sharks evolve	**435 mya** First bony fish and first land plants and animals appear	**408 mya** Fishes diversify, first insects and amphibians appear	**360 mya** Golden Age of Sharks, first reptiles appear
Trilobites resembled bugs, but some grew more than 2 feet (60 cm) long.	*Sharks with jaws may have evolved from jawless thelodonts such as the one shown here.*	*As life blossomed on land, the sea featured bony fish such as spiny* Nostolepsis *swimming with sharks.*	*Some modern sharks have spines in front of their dorsal fins, like* Ctenacanthus *did.*	*No one knows how the scissor-tooth shark used its weird whorls of teeth.*

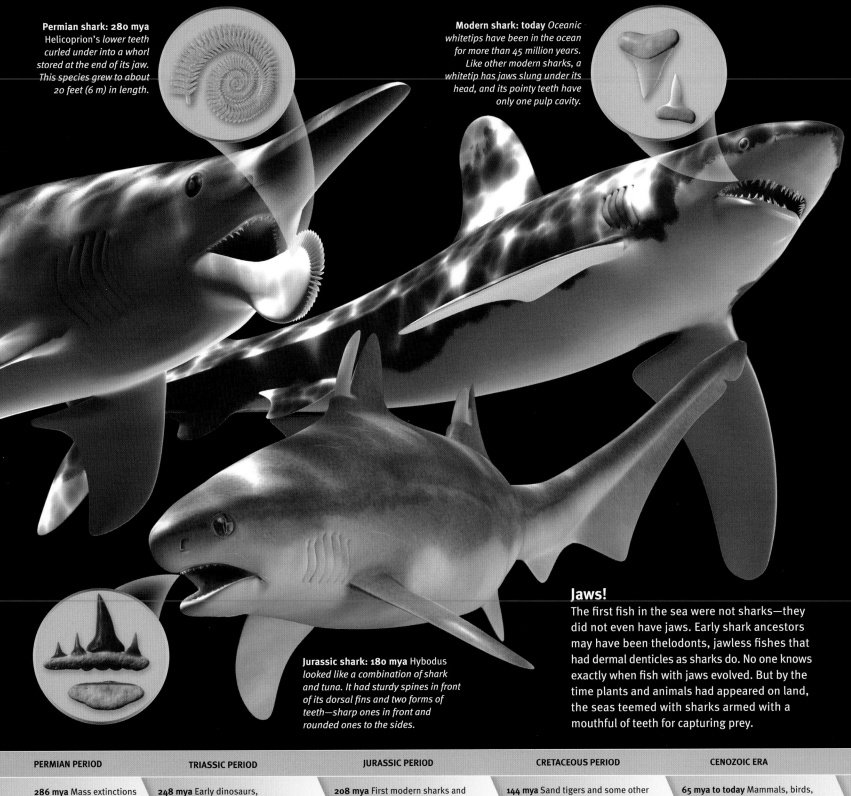

Permian shark: 280 mya Helicoprion's *lower teeth curled under into a whorl stored at the end of its jaw. This species grew to about 20 feet (6 m) in length.*

Modern shark: today *Oceanic whitetips have been in the ocean for more than 45 million years. Like other modern sharks, a whitetip has jaws slung under its head, and its pointy teeth have only one pulp cavity.*

Jurassic shark: 180 mya Hybodus *looked like a combination of shark and tuna. It had sturdy spines in front of its dorsal fins and two forms of teeth—sharp ones in front and rounded ones to the sides.*

Jaws!

The first fish in the sea were not sharks—they did not even have jaws. Early shark ancestors may have been thelodonts, jawless fishes that had dermal denticles as sharks do. No one knows exactly when fish with jaws evolved. But by the time plants and animals had appeared on land, the seas teemed with sharks armed with a mouthful of teeth for capturing prey.

PERMIAN PERIOD	TRIASSIC PERIOD	JURASSIC PERIOD	CRETACEOUS PERIOD	CENOZOIC ERA
286 mya Mass extinctions both on land and in seas	**248 mya** Early dinosaurs, mammals, and marine reptiles	**208 mya** First modern sharks and rays, mass extinctions in seas	**144 mya** Sand tigers and some other modern shark lineages, first birds	**65 mya to today** Mammals, birds, and flowering plants diversify
Permian rivers were home to eel-like sharks such as Xenacanthus (below left). Dimetrodon (below right) roamed the land.	*Nothosaurus was a reptile with webbed toes and needle-like teeth. It may have hunted fish in the ocean.*	*Rays may have evolved from a flattened shark such as Protospinax.*	*Tyrannosaurus (below left) and other dinosaurs ruled the land. Top ocean predators included Cretoxyrhina (below right), a relative of the great white.*	*Gigantic Megalodon (below) dominated the oceans. On land, ancestors of modern humans (below right) evolved.*

Record-breaking
Sharks

Some sharks really go to extremes. They grow longer than a semitruck, swim faster than a dolphin, or survive in the murkiest depths. Nearly two million years ago prehistoric seas were home to Megalodon, the most massive predatory shark that ever lived. This whale-hunting monster had a mouthful of giant 7-inch (18-cm) teeth and could weigh as much as four lumbering African elephants—an astounding 52 tons (47 t). Relatives of all today's shark families lived alongside Megalodon, with features that helped them endure through the ages. Although Megalodon went extinct, other species of its time paved the way for the many different shark lifestyles we see in our oceans.

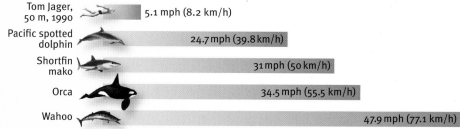

Tom Jager, 50 m, 1990	5.1 mph (8.2 km/h)
Pacific spotted dolphin	24.7 mph (39.8 km/h)
Shortfin mako	31 mph (50 km/h)
Orca	34.5 mph (55.5 km/h)
Wahoo	47.9 mph (77.1 km/h)

How fast?
The sailfish can leap from the water at 68 miles per hour (109 km/h), but another bony fish, the wahoo, holds the underwater swimming record, with a speed of nearly 48 miles per hour (77 km/h). The fastest of all sharks, the shortfin mako, has been clocked at 31 miles per hour (50 km/h).

How deep?
Sharks survive in warm tide pools at the sea's surface, in frigid waters more than 12,000 feet (3,660 m) deep, and everywhere in between.

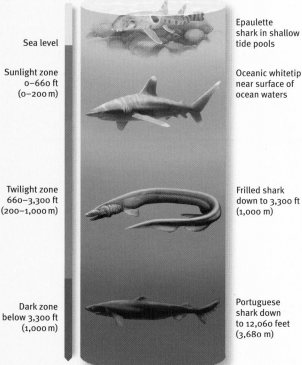

Sea level	Epaulette shark in shallow tide pools
Sunlight zone 0–660 ft (0–200 m)	Oceanic whitetip near surface of ocean waters
Twilight zone 660–3,300 ft (200–1,000 m)	Frilled shark down to 3,300 ft (1,000 m)
Dark zone below 3,300 ft (1,000 m)	Portuguese shark down to 12,060 feet (3,680 m)

Dwarf lanternshark *The smallest shark is probably the dwarf lanternshark, with some pregnant females measuring only 7.5 inches (19 cm) long.*

How old?
Sharks live much longer than most other fish. One shark, the spiny dogfish, can survive for 70 years—if it stays clear of predators and fishing nets.

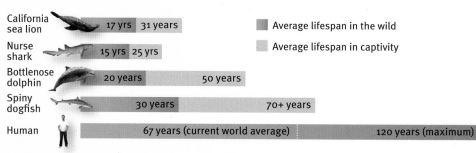

California sea lion	17 yrs	31 years
Nurse shark	15 yrs	25 yrs
Bottlenose dolphin	20 years	50 years
Spiny dogfish	30 years	70+ years
Human	67 years (current world average)	120 years (maximum)

■ Average lifespan in the wild
■ Average lifespan in captivity

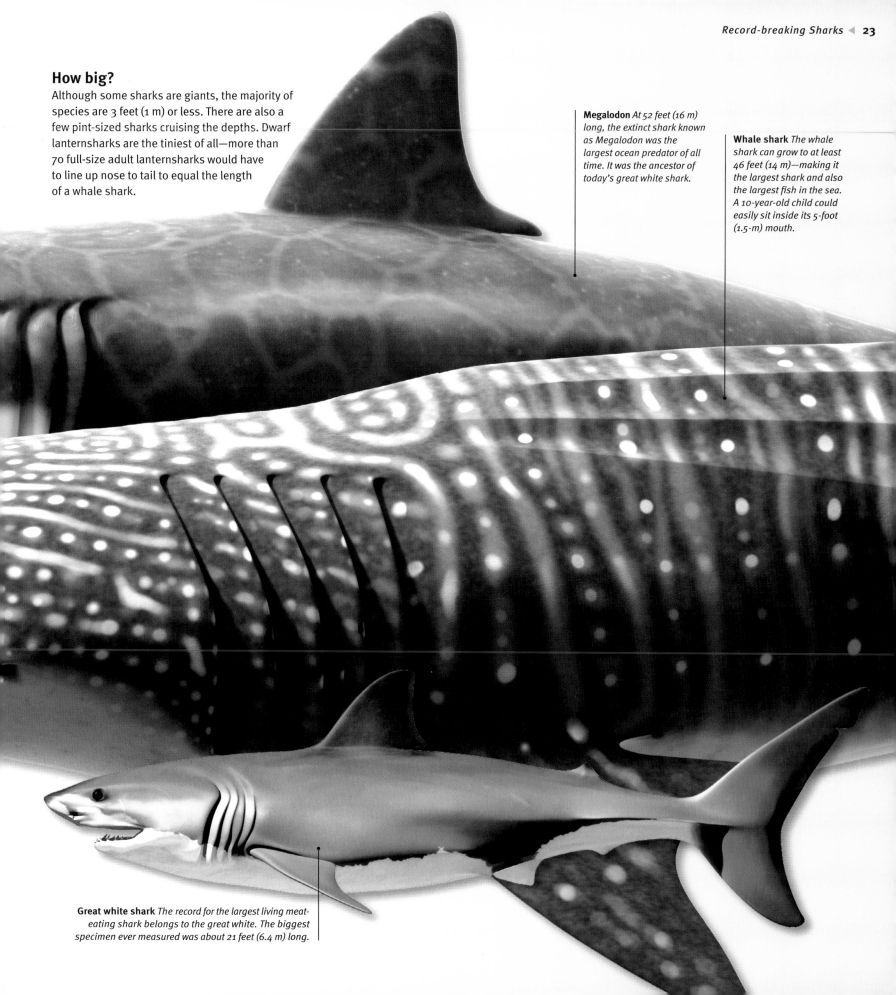

How big?

Although some sharks are giants, the majority of species are 3 feet (1 m) or less. There are also a few pint-sized sharks cruising the depths. Dwarf lanternsharks are the tiniest of all—more than 70 full-size adult lanternsharks would have to line up nose to tail to equal the length of a whale shark.

Megalodon *At 52 feet (16 m) long, the extinct shark known as Megalodon was the largest ocean predator of all time. It was the ancestor of today's great white shark.*

Whale shark *The whale shark can grow to at least 46 feet (14 m)—making it the largest shark and also the largest fish in the sea. A 10-year-old child could easily sit inside its 5-foot (1.5-m) mouth.*

Great white shark *The record for the largest living meat-eating shark belongs to the great white. The biggest specimen ever measured was about 21 feet (6.4 m) long.*

Seizing Prey
On the Hunt

Sharks are masters of the hunt. Fast swimmers such as makos and blue sharks chase down prey in a flash of speed, while stealthy great whites, bull sharks, and tiger sharks stalk and kill with a fierce slash of their jaws. Huge whale sharks can suck in thousands of tiny krill in a single gulp from below. Bottom-dwellers such as angel sharks and wobbegongs lie in wait on the seafloor, surprising prey with an ambush attack. The secret weapon of a thresher shark is its long tail. Using the tail like a hockey stick, the thresher herds up a school of fish, then strikes a massive blow. The stunned victims become the thresher's meal.

Biting a baitball!
When dolphins herd prey fish into densely packed clumps, sharks often join in on the feast. These bronze whalers are primed to snatch a stomach full of food from the whirling baitball.

A tiger's stripes *Tiger sharks can grow to more than 15 feet (4.5 m) long. They get their name from the dark stripes on their brown skin. The stripes fade with age and may vanish in very large adults.*

Ambush predator
Resting almost motionless and superbly camouflaged on the sandy seafloor, an alert Pacific angel shark waits to pounce on a passing fish.

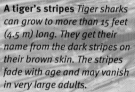

Forager
A longnose sawshark may use its tooth-studded snout to strike fish or stir up prey from the bottom. The long barbels that hang from its snout could help detect prey.

Group hunter
Thresher sharks sometimes hunt in pairs. While one shark performs the powerful tail slap, the other picks off fish that are too stunned to swim.

Chaser
Porbeagle sharks are very fast swimmers and will often chase their meal. In cool parts of the ocean they race after schools of herring and other small fish.

Loggerhead turtle *Loggerheads can weigh more than 200 pounds (90 kg). They hunt underwater for crabs, shrimps, and other sea life. When they swim up to the surface to breathe, they become more vulnerable to attack.*

Eye protection *An extra eyelid called a nictitating membrane closes over the tiger shark's eyes during the attack on the turtle. The membrane protects the eyes from being damaged by the struggling victim.*

Jagged edge *A tiger shark's serrated teeth are excellent tools for shearing through a turtle's flesh. They act like saws as the shark shakes its head from side to side.*

Seagrass bed *Beds of seagrass grow in sunlit shallows. Small marine creatures such as fish, crabs, and snails live among the submerged blades of grass, where they can hide from predators.*

Sudden strike

A loggerhead sea turtle searching for crabs in the shallows is a tempting target for a hungry tiger shark. Eyeing its prey from below, the shark closes in slowly, then attacks in a sudden rush. As its huge jaws clamp down, the tiger shark's curved, serrated teeth are already ripping the doomed turtle's flesh or sawing through its shell.

Famine or
Feast

For a shark, hunting is all about hunger. When its stomach is empty, a shark may spend hours or days in search of food, ever alert and ready to strike. But when the shark has eaten its fill, the search for prey stops while the shark slowly digests the meal. Fast swimmers such as makos can gobble more than their body weight in food every month, while a sluggish sandbar shark may eat only the fishy equivalent of a small hamburger every day or two. A great white shark can gulp down a whole seal in an hour, but when the feast is over, it may not hunt again for a month.

IF IT FITS, EAT IT

When scientists capture sharks for study, they check out what the shark has been eating. Tiger sharks are expert hunters but are also scavengers and will eat anything they can swallow. Shoes, garbage from cruise ships, buckets, trash cans, tar paper—even a suit of armor—all have been found in tiger shark stomachs.

Ocean ecology

An ocean food web starts with phytoplankton, which use sunlight to produce their own food. Zooplankton eat phytoplankton, small fish eat zooplankton, and so on up to sharks at the top of the web.

Great white shark

Seal

Salmon

Soupfin shark

Squid

Herring

Phytoplankton

Zooplankton

Undersea banquet

An ocean food web can feed only a handful of top predators such as sharks because predators need to eat many smaller prey to survive. When millions of market squid gather to find mates, blue sharks eat the easy way—they swim through the gleaming squid with their jaws opening and closing, swallowing huge mouthfuls of the squid soup until their stomachs are stuffed.

Producing the Next
Generation

Making a new generation may be a shark's greatest challenge. To begin with, sharks must grow for 10 or 20 years before they can mate. Then they have only a few, large young. In most species females have two wombs, or uteri, where the mother carries her unborn young for up to two years while they develop into pint-sized copies of their parents. Before birth, baby sharks get food in different ways—some from a large sac of yolk, others by eating extra eggs. Some species receive nourishment from the mother's bloodstream via a placenta, like a developing human baby does. Unborn sand tiger sharks become cannibals. The first one in each uterus to grow to about 4 inches (10 cm) long uses its tiny teeth to gobble up its smaller littermates.

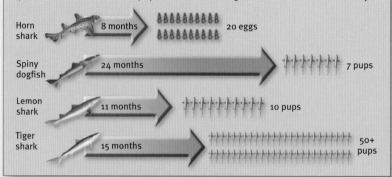

COMPARING LITTERS

Compared to many other animals, sharks have few young and spend a long time making them. The time an animal spends developing before birth is known as its gestation period. Most sharks have gestation periods lasting a year or two. The number of pups in each litter ranges from two to more than fifty.

Horn shark — 8 months — 20 eggs

Spiny dogfish — 24 months — 7 pups

Lemon shark — 11 months — 10 pups

Tiger shark — 15 months — 50+ pups

Growing a shark

A shark begins life as a microscopic cell that forms after a sperm from a male fertilizes an egg in a female. Step by step, its tissues and organs form and begin to function. This image sequence shows how a shortspine spurdog shark takes shape during the two years it spends inside its mother. After birth, 10 or 15 more years will pass before the shark is ready to produce a new generation.

1 **Fertilized egg** *After the shortspine spurdog's egg is fertilized, it has two main parts—a large supply of yolk and a plate of cells called a blastodisc. A tiny shark embryo is beginning to develop.*

A shark is born

A baby shark grows inside one of its mother's two uteri. In some species, such as this lemon shark, a placenta develops from each embryo's yolk sac. This sac is connected to the mother's bloodstream, which nourishes the young shark. Eventually the pup is born tail-first. In the photo the newborn pup is still attached to its mother by an umbilical cord, but the cord will soon break and the pup will swim away.

2 **Building backbone** *Cells in the blastodisc move into new positions, creating a fold that will become the baby shark's cartilage spine. Soon other cells will develop into muscles and organs such as the heart.*

3 **A brain begins** *The shark embryo is growing longer as more body parts develop. At one end of the spine the skull-like cranium has formed. Inside the cranium the embryo's tiny brain is taking shape.*

Egg-laying sharks

Not all sharks give birth to live pups. In some species the eggs are protected inside a tough case that contains yolk for the embryo. The mother lays her egg cases on the seafloor or attaches them to a rock, and the pups hatch later on their own. The empty egg cases often wash up on beaches and are sometimes called "mermaid's purses."

Horn shark A horn shark egg case twists like a corkscrew. The twists help keep it wedged in rock crevices.

Australian draftboard shark The hard surface of this egg case helps protect against predators such as sea snails.

Catshark A tiny developing catshark spends about two years inside its see-through egg case.

Swellshark After many months inside its purse-shaped egg case, a swellshark pup is breaking free.

5 Fully formed *As months pass, the embryo develops into a complex fetus that looks like a miniature shark. The yolk sac shrinks as the little shark uses yolk for food.*

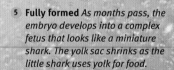

4 Yolk supply *The embryo is beginning to look like a fish. A stalk connects it to the yolk sac. Blood vessels inside the stalk transfer yolk to the embryo.*

6 Newborn pup *Finally the young shortspine spurdog is born. About 1 foot (30 cm) long, it is ready to hunt and quickly swims away from its mother to pursue a shrimp—its first meal in the sea.*

Ocean
Vagabonds

Some sharks are incredible long-distance travelers. Moving like submarines on a mission, they migrate along coasts or through the open sea—leaving one place, swimming to a new destination, then retracing their path months or years later. The search for a mate can lead a shark to faraway waters where males and females meet up every year or two. Some sharks also migrate when the ocean temperature changes as summer or winter approaches. Many kinds of prey migrate when seasons shift, so the sharks simply follow along. But for makos and some other shark species, water that is too cool or too warm is a mortal enemy. Their vast journeys are voyages of survival.

Migration mysteries

Swimming in schools or traveling solo, many sharks migrate far and wide. But until recently, most shark migrations were cloaked in mystery. Scientists can now attach a little device known as a satellite tag to the shark. As the shark swims, the tag sends signals to a satellite orbiting far above Earth. The satellite relays the signal back down to the scientists' computers, allowing them to track the shark's journey. Such studies have revealed far-flung voyages of 5,000 miles (8,000 km) or more.

Sandbar shark *When female sandbar sharks are about to give birth, they migrate far away from where male sandbars are hunting. Otherwise, the males might eat the newborn pups! Baby sandbar sharks zigzag around their nursery grounds looking for food, covering up to 20 miles (30 km) in a day.*

Blacktip shark *Speedy blacktip sharks migrate in large groups, swimming south along the coast as summer turns to autumn, then turning back north as winter warms to spring. Female blacktips travel to shallow coastal nursery grounds where their newborns will find plenty of food and meet fewer predators.*

NORTH
AMERICA

New York ●

*Atlantic
Ocean*

Houston ●

*Gulf of
Mexico*

*Caribbean
Sea*

Caracas ●

SOUTH
AMERICA

*Pacific
Ocean*

Shark travels

➡ Basking shark migration

➡ Mako shark migration

➡ Blue shark migration

➡ Blacktip shark migration

➡ Sandbar shark migration

▬ Nurse shark distribution (no migration)

Basking shark *Satellite tags shot from a harpoon gun solved a shark mystery. In summer, basking sharks loll at the surface near the coast, filtering plankton from seawater. As plankton there become scarce in winter, the huge sharks disappear. At one time, people supposed that baskers hibernate like bears in winter. But tag signals revealed that the sharks migrated south to deep water, where plankton remain plentiful during the colder months.*

ASIA

London

Paris

EUROPE

Madrid

Mediterranean Sea

Rabat

Mako shark *Fitted with a satellite tag, this shortfin mako can be tracked for months. Makos migrate individually. They spend summer in the coastal waters of the northeastern United States. As the weather cools, they make marathon journeys all the way to South America and Africa.*

AFRICA

Atlantic Ocean

Dakar

Blue shark *Blue sharks spend much of their life migrating, chasing fish or squid through cool regions of the sea. In the Atlantic they travel with powerful ocean currents that flow clockwise in a rough circle from west to east and back again. Fishing boats sometimes target large schools of migrating blue sharks.*

Nurse shark *Not all sharks make long migrations. Nurse sharks live in shallow tropical seas (shaded green on this map). Like many other sluggish sharks, they are homebodies and never stray far from their birthplace.*

Shark Relatives

Flat Cousins

Rays and skates, guitarfish and sawfish—these shark cousins are known as batoids and live mostly near the seafloor. Like sharks, they have a skeleton of cartilage, but the body is flattened and the gill slits are on the underside. Broad pectoral fins sweep back from the head. These winglike fins allow batoids to fly through the water as they hunt clams, shrimps, or other prey. Some batoid species are dull gray or brownish, but many sport bold stripes, spots, or jagged blotches. Odd as these "birds of the seas" might seem, they are found all over the ocean world.

Manta ray *Also known as the devil ray, the enormous manta ray is a filter feeder. As a manta swims near the surface, the fleshy flaps on either side of its snout help direct tiny prey and water into its huge open mouth. Bristles in front of the gills trap the food.*

Rough skate *Nubby rows and patches of thorns give the rough skate its name. Rough skates typically live in the cool ocean depths below 660 feet (200 m), where they spend much of the time partially buried in sand.*

Bowmouth guitarfish *With the head of a ray and the tail of a shark, a guitarfish resembles a guitar or banjo. The bowmouth guitarfish has spiky thorns along the ridge of its back. This bottom-dweller uses its rows of ridged teeth for crushing crabs and other shellfish.*

How a ray swims

Rays and skates swim by flapping their wings up and down as birds do. Guitarfish and sawfish move like sharks, by flexing their tail from side to side.

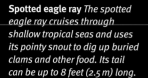

Spotted eagle ray *The spotted eagle ray cruises through shallow tropical seas and uses its pointy snout to dig up buried clams and other food. Its tail can be up to 8 feet (2.5 m) long.*

Batoids great and small

Rays and skates have a round or heart-shaped disk and a slender, whiplike tail. Many species are armed with thorns or spines for defense. Guitarfish and sawfish combine a batoid's flat disk with the tail of a shark. The disk of a manta ray (center) may be more than 22 feet (6.7 m) wide, and sawfish can be 20 feet (6 m) long. Other rays are smaller, and some skates are not much larger than a dinner plate.

Smalltooth sawfish *Using its remarkable tooth-studded snout, a smalltooth sawfish can stir up sediments and disable small prey. Some individuals have as many as 34 pairs of teeth on the "saw."*

Pacific electric ray *With two special organs in the disk near the head, an electric ray produces an electric current that can stun an unsuspecting fish. Before the prey revives, the ray swims atop and devours it.*

CURIOUS CHIMAERAS

Chimaeras are rather mysterious relatives of sharks and rays. Found mostly in the deep sea, they have a cartilage skeleton, but in the place of upper teeth they have a parrot-like beak. These unusual fish also have only a single, covered opening to their gills.

Elephantfish The elephantfish has a long, flaring snout equipped with sensory organs that help it find worms, crabs, and other prey buried in the bottom.

White-spotted ratfish This ratfish lives along seacoasts. Despite its pretty eyes, its venom-filled dorsal spine can inflict a painful wound.

Spookfish The snout of this spookfish works much like a flexible antenna. It detects electric fields produced by crabs and other prey.

Other Superpredators
Competition

When it comes to finding food in the sea, other top predators rival even the mightiest of sharks. Some of the fiercest shark competitors are orcas. Also known as killer whales, these aggressive speedsters have long, backward-curving teeth for catching many types of prey—fish, squid, sea turtles, massive blue whales, and even sharks. In all, an adult orca may eat 500 pounds (225 kg) of food each day. Even the most powerful great white is no match for an orca, which can grow to more than 30 feet (9.1 m) and weigh more than 6 tons (5.4 t).

Spyhopping *Orcas sometimes raise their upper body out of the water and look around. This behavior is called spyhopping, but no one knows why orcas do it.*

Shark rivals
Sea lions, dolphins, supersize fish such as giant groupers, and even saltwater crocodiles are among the ocean's top predators. They cruise the seas, often on the hunt for the same prey as sharks.

Steller sea lion These blubbery but strong marine mammals are meat-eaters, catching rockfish, pollock, and other fish as well as skates and small sharks.

Bottlenose dolphin The bottlenose uses its dozens of cone-shaped teeth to spear squid, octopuses, and small fish before gulping down the prey whole.

Goliath grouper The slow-moving goliath grouper has a big mouth but tiny teeth. It eats mostly crabs and shrimps, plus bottom-hugging creatures such as catfish and stingrays.

Saltwater crocodile A crocodile traps prey underwater in its viselike jaws. Land animals soon drown. Aquatic prey, including small bull sharks, suffocate as they cannot keep swimming.

SHARK DEFENSES

Sharks employ some intriguing methods of self-defense. Many species use their jaws and teeth to counterattack, or else swiftly flee when a predator strikes. Others are protected by camouflage, sharp spines, or the curious ability to swell up and appear larger.

Spiky spines Only about 20 inches (50 cm) long, the Caribbean rough shark fends off predators with sharp spines in front of its two dorsal fins.

Safety in numbers Whitetip reef sharks huddle together under coral formations or rock ledges where larger predators cannot easily attack.

Shark for lunch *With its muscular body and huge, oily liver, a great white shark makes a nutritious meal. Several orcas may share in the feast.*

Powerful pod

Orcas live and hunt in groups called pods. An orca pod can mean big trouble for a great white shark. Near the Farallon Islands off California, scientists watched the members of a pod toss a great white into the air like a beach ball before killing and eating it. Given its size and power, even a single orca is an awesome challenge for a lone great white.

Orca attack *Like the great white, orcas attack from below in a sudden burst of speed. They have been clocked at 30 miles per hour (48 km/h). Larger individuals lead the charge, with smaller ones joining in later.*

Puffy protection When a predator threatens, a swell shark swallows water and puffs up—sometimes becoming twice its normal size.

Cryptic coloring Adult zebra sharks are spotted, but the young have wavy stripes that blend in with the dappled sunlit water of the shallows.

Shark Attacks

Dark circling fins, vicious teeth slashing, the ocean swirling red with blood—this is the terrifying reputation of sharks. Most shark teeth are so razor sharp, they can easily rip through human flesh. On very rare occasions large sharks will target humans as prey, but strange as it may seem, most shark attacks are simply mistakes. If a blacktip hunting close to shore senses vibrations in the water and sees a flash of movement, it may rush in and grab a foot instead of the fish it expected. Murky water or the dim light of dawn or dusk makes an attack more likely. And even a resting shark can be spurred to attack if a curious or careless diver comes too close.

Dolphin

Marlin

Basking shark

Manta ray

What are the odds?

The odds of a shark attack are extremely small—only about one in twelve million. Swimmers are five times more likely to drown or suffer injury in some other way. Each year there are about 75 unprovoked shark attacks, and most victims survive.

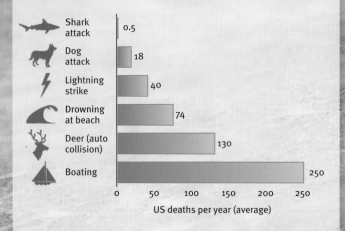

	US deaths per year (average)
Shark attack	0.5
Dog attack	18
Lightning strike	40
Drowning at beach	74
Deer (auto collision)	130
Boating	250

SHARK—OR NOT?

A dorsal fin slicing through the water is not always cause for a shark alarm. Dolphins, marlins, gentle basking sharks, and several other marine creatures have dorsal fins that sometimes break the surface. Even a manta ray's "wing" can look like a shark's dorsal fin.

Man-eater!

Many experts believe that bull sharks are the most dangerous sharks. Like great whites and tiger sharks, they are aggressive and hunt large prey. Many sharks will retreat if a person kicks or punches back in self-defense. Not the bull shark—it comes back again and again, focused squarely on its target. And once its jaws close on a victim, a bull shark may hold on even while rescuers attack it.

Danger zone *Bull sharks nearly always attack humans close to shore. They can lurk in tropical lagoons, river shallows, even in narrow canals lined with homes. Lone surfers, splashing swimmers, and divers may all become tempting potential prey.*

Safe
Swimming

In the sea, people are visitors to a shark's world. Even though attacks are rare, shark-smart swimmers can take simple measures to limit their risk. It is wise to stay ashore at dawn and dusk, when sharks hunt actively. Sharks can detect even small prey movements and have a keen sense of smell, so where a shark may come calling, swimmers should avoid vigorous splashing and stay out of the water if they are bleeding. A passing school of baitfish or a fishing boat can also lure sharks close to shore. A sharp-eyed shark may even investigate shiny jewelry or clothing that contrasts with a person's skin.

At ease *If people stay far enough away from a shark, it does not feel threatened. It usually ignores them and swims normally, holding its body in a straight line.*

Being shark savvy

"Man-eaters" such as great whites, tiger sharks, and bull sharks are always dangerous to humans, but most sharks usually pose no risk to people who keep a respectful distance. When a careless person does venture too close, a shark may use body language to signal "Back off!" The display is a warning that the shark perceives the person as a serious threat—and may soon launch an attack to protect itself.

Lucky escape
Surviving a shark attack can take luck, pluck, or both. Some victims drive off aggressive sharks with swift punches to the eye or nose. The owner of this surfboard was extremely lucky. He had teeth marks in his wetsuit but escaped without a scratch. All the shark got was a crunchy mouthful of board.

Ignoring the warning *The scuba diver is wearing a shark tooth pendant as a lucky charm, a tradition that began in Hawaii, where sharks are revered as powerful spirits. The pendant will not be enough to protect her, however, if she persists in getting her close-up of the shark. She needs to respond to the shark's warning display and leave the area, or the shark may mount a defensive attack.*

PRECAUTIONS

In some coastal regions dangerous sharks are common. To help prevent unwanted encounters, authorities may order shark-spotting patrols or place a fencelike net in the water. Divers and scientists can use cages or other protection to keep sharks at bay.

Shark patrol Near many popular beaches, helicopter crews fly low over the sea, on the lookout for dorsal fins or other signs of sharks.

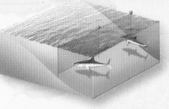

Beach mesh Long nets set up just beyond the breaking waves can prevent stealth attacks by sharks such as great whites. A shark caught in the mesh may suffocate and die.

Protective clothing Steel-mesh suits allow scientists to safely study large sharks. They also allow photographers to snap thrilling close-ups.

Distress signals *This cornered shark is trying to warn off the scuba diver. The arched back, lowered pectoral fins, sideways tail, raised snout, and wagging head—all are signals that the shark is feeling uneasy.*

Sharks
In Danger

All over the world ocean, sharks are under siege. Every year the nets and hooks of commercial fishing fleets haul up 100 million sharks, and about 70 million more die after their fins are sliced off. Human activities are polluting and even destroying coral reefs and mangrove shallows—and with them go the homes of shark pups. To make matters worse, many sharks must grow for 10 or 20 years before they can mate and produce more young. This fact is grim news for sharks, because it means that many more die than are born, so the numbers of these great hunters keep dropping. With so many top predators disappearing, the ocean's natural balance is also in danger.

SHARKS UNDER THREAT

The World Conservation Union monitors threats to sharks. Critically Endangered species are in danger of going extinct very soon. Species that are listed as Endangered or Vulnerable may have more time, but they also are at serious risk.

Striped smoothhound *Critically Endangered* Fishing nets have captured many thousands of these small sharks. They have all but disappeared from their home waters off the southeast coast of South America.

Daggernose shark *Critically Endangered* Experts are trying to educate local fishers about the looming threat to the daggernose, but the species has almost vanished off Venezuela and nearby countries where it once flourished.

Smoothback angel shark *Endangered* Trawl nets that scrape along the bottom of the sea often scoop up smoothback angel sharks, and nets set for other fish kill many more as bycatch.

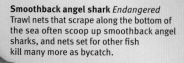

Sand tiger shark *Vulnerable* A female sand tiger has only two pups every other year. Because so few young are born, losing even a few adults can seriously deplete a sand tiger population.

Tangled up *Commercial fishing boats often use strong monofilament nylon nets that may extend for more than 30 miles (50 km). Sharks such as this pelagic thresher may not see the fatal net until it is too late.*

Lured by prey *Sharks may wind up in nets while they are pursuing prey such as tuna and mackerel. Even if a netted shark survives, it may be killed aboard ship or have its valuable fins cut off.*

Caught in the trap

A fish is called bycatch when it is caught with gear set for a different species. Countless sharks die when they are taken as bycatch, either entangled in a fishing net or dangling from a hook set for another type of fish. A few nations have laws forbidding the capture of endangered or threatened sharks, but bycatch is permitted. This legal loophole means that many protected sharks die anyway.

Doomed hammerhead *Fishing fleets often operate on the open ocean where their vast nets and longlines may capture a variety of large sharks, including many hammerheads. Hopelessly caught in the net's mesh, this smooth hammerhead has little chance of escaping.*

Death watch *An entangled shark thrashes wildly, but it cannot swim. With seawater barely moving across its gills, it does not get enough oxygen. Even though the shark is submerged, it will slowly suffocate and die.*

Fins for soup

The fishing industry makes plenty of money selling shark fins, which are used in Asian countries for a luxury soup. After the fins are sliced off, the shark usually is tossed back into the sea. Unable to swim, it sinks to the ocean floor and drowns.

Predator Protection
Saving Sharks

With sharks under threat, many people are trying to ensure that these ocean superstars survive. In much of the world, it is now illegal to harm vulnerable species such as the great white and whale shark. Conservation groups are urging governments to protect all sharks from overfishing and finning. Other programs are working to protect and restore habitats that are nurseries for baby sharks. Scientists are using high-tech electronic gear to solve many puzzles about sharks, including how they navigate and make their long migrations through the seas. And public aquariums and adventure tours are allowing millions of people to learn about the undersea lives of sharks. These efforts and more aim to provide sharks with a lifeline to the future.

In captivity
Public aquariums play an important role in educating people about the vulnerability and decline of sharks. Large sand tigers like this one have all but disappeared from the waters of Australia and are rare in many other parts of the world ocean.

Lemon sharks *Mother lemon sharks give birth to their pups in the shallows near mangrove forests. Food is plentiful there, and the baby sharks are protected from larger sharks, which must stay in deeper water. Young lemon sharks may live in their nursery grounds for several years.*

Shark tourism
In some places sharks have become an important tourist attraction, with people traveling from around the world to dive with them. The success of the shark-dive industry proves that sharks are more valuable alive than dead.

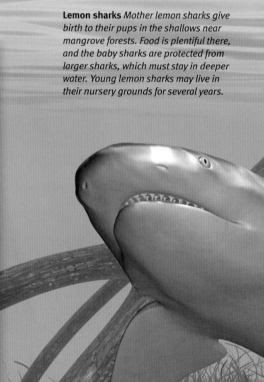

Pup prey *Many species of crabs, shrimps, and small fish shelter among the submerged roots of mangroves. They are an abundant food supply for lemon shark pups.*

Shared nursery *The young of many larger coastal fish use the mangroves as a nursery area. Some of these juvenile fish may become meals for birds that hunt in the mangroves. Here an egret is snacking on a small mullet.*

Home for baby sharks

Efforts are under way to save mangrove forests—rich habitats at the edge of the sea where many sharks get their start in life. More than half of the world's original mangrove area has disappeared, and much of what remains is under threat from development. Mangrove trees create a haven for many aquatic creatures. Their rotting leaves provide food for snails, worms, and other small creatures, which in turn are eaten by young fish and crabs. The small fish and crabs become the prey of waterbirds, larger fish, and baby sharks.

A tangle of roots *Mangrove trees grow in the shallows of estuaries, where freshwater from rivers meets seawater. Prop roots support the trunk and branches above the water.*

Sea level

SUNLIGHT ZONE

660 ft (200 m)

Locator map The green shading on this map of the world shows you where the featured sharks live.

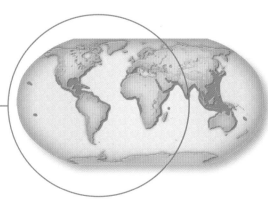

HAMMERHEADS: THE FACTS

SPECIES: 9 species, all in the family Sphyrnidae

GROUP: Ground sharks (order Carcharhiniformes)

DIET: Fish, squid, octopuses, rays, crustaceans

HABITAT: Warm coastal waters

REPRODUCTION: Live-bearer with litters of 20–50 pups; embryos nourished via placenta; gestation 10 months

CONSERVATION STATUS: Great hammerhead Endangered; golden hammerhead Vulnerable; scalloped, smooth, winghead, and scalloped bonnethead Near Threatened

Fast facts Fast facts at your fingertips give you essential information about the sharks.

TWILIGHT ZONE

Depth bar This depth bar indicates how far beneath the ocean's surface the sharks can be found.

3,300 ft (1,000 m)

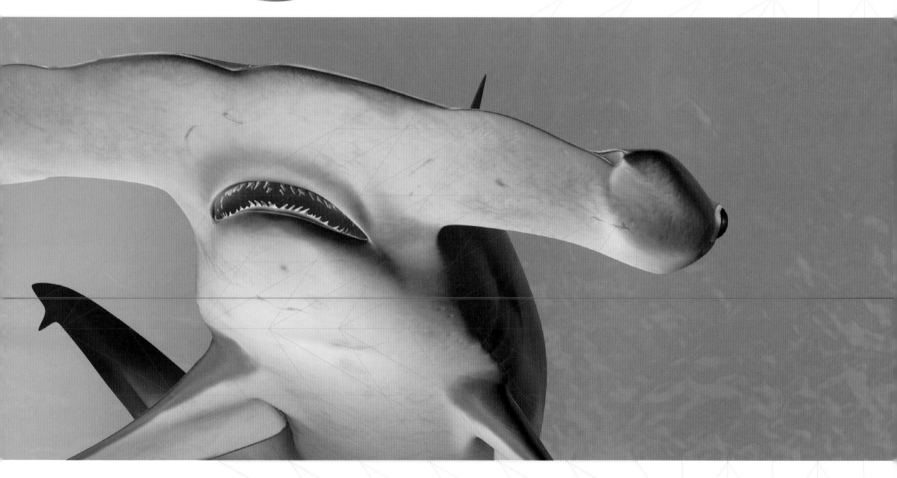

Sea level

SUNLIGHT ZONE

660 ft (200 m)

775 ft (240 m)

TWILIGHT ZONE

3,300 ft (1,000 m)

GREAT WHITE SHARK: THE FACTS

ALSO KNOWN AS: White pointer, man-eater shark

SPECIES: *Carcharodon carcharias*

GROUP: Mackerel sharks (order Lamniformes)

DIET: Fish, other sharks, marine mammals such as seals

HABITAT: In warm months, near coasts and islands, especially around seal colonies; open ocean in winter

REPRODUCTION: Live-bearer with litters of 2–14 pups; embryos eat undeveloped eggs; gestation 12 months

CONSERVATION STATUS: Vulnerable; protected in many places

Great White Shark

Supercharged

Roaming almost the whole world ocean, the great white shark rules as the mightiest shark of all. Like its ancestor Megalodon, the great white is awe-inspiring—with massive jaws full of huge triangular teeth, it may grow to an amazing 20 feet (6 m) or more. Using color vision and other keen senses, a great white sneaks up on prey, then rushes in for the kill with explosive speed. A young great white may catch fish or other sharks, but as it grows to full size it targets ever-larger prey, including elephant seals, sea lions, dolphins, and small whales. Anything that looks like prey—including an unlucky human—may become the great white's next meal.

Seal or surfer?
Research shows that great whites can see the outlines of objects that resemble their prey. From below a seal looks like a dark oval with legs—and so does a surfer on a surfboard.

Tail action *A great white uses its keen senses to guide its slow approach. When the time is right, its muscular tail rockets the massive shark toward its unsuspecting prey.*

Teeth shown actual size

Typical jaw width 28 inches (71 cm)

Great whites up close
An adult great white's jaws may gape more than 2 feet (60 cm) wide. With this huge maw the shark can engulf bulky food items such as the tail of an elephant seal, a whole pelican, or an impressive chunk from a surfboard. Teeth the size shown here would belong to a 16-foot (5-m) great white—an average-size adult female.

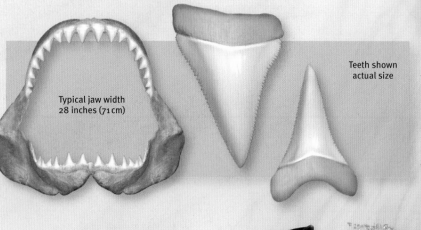

10-year-old boy 4.5 ft (1.4 m)

Average female great white 16 ft (5 m)

Unguarded moment *Northern elephant seals are mammals and must breathe at the surface. For a few seconds, these hefty, agile swimmers become clumsy and vulnerable—and a great white may seize the moment to strike.*

Bite and spit *Great whites use a bite-and-spit strategy to capture northern elephant seals. After its ferocious first bite rips the seal's tail, the shark lets go. As the seal dies from blood loss, the shark returns to feed. A great white may carry a smaller victim in its tightly clenched jaws, waiting for the prey to die before devouring it.*

Jaw-cam *This seal-hunting scene is shown from inside the mouth of a second great white, which has opened its awesome jaws and is about to join the attack.*

Seal meal

A busy seal or sea lion rookery is a waiting banquet for great white sharks. Although several sharks may arrive for the feast, only the largest take center stage. In a stealth attack from below, the dominant great whites launch a fast and furious attack. As the waters fill with the blood of dying prey, smaller individuals lurk at the fringes, ready to gobble leftovers. They eat only when their larger cousins have had enough.

Sea level

SUNLIGHT ZONE

66o ft (200 m)

TWILIGHT ZONE

3,300 ft (1,000 m)

4,000 ft (1,200 m)

DARK ZONE

6,600 ft (2,000 m)

GREENLAND SLEEPER: THE FACTS

SPECIES: *Somniosus microcephalus*

GROUP: Dogfish sharks (order Squaliformes)

DIET: Fish, seals and sea lions, seabirds, giant squid and octopuses, shellfish, dead whales, drowned land animals

HABITAT: Cold water over continental shelves and slopes

REPRODUCTION: Live-bearer with litters of about 10 pups; embryos nourished by yolk in eggs; gestation unknown

CONSERVATION STATUS: Near Threatened

Greenland Sleeper
Cold and Deep

Imagine Inuit fishermen in the icy Arctic huffing and puffing as they tug ashore a flabby shark measuring more than 20 feet (6 m) and weighing more than 2,400 pounds (1,100 kg). The Inuit supposedly used seal intestines to lure in their catch—a Greenland sleeper shark, the largest fish in the Arctic. There are several species of sleeper sharks. The Pacific sleeper haunts cold, deep Pacific waters, and another giant lives in the waters off Antarctica. Sleepers both hunt live prey and scavenge dead remains. Scientists have found an amazing assortment of items in their stomachs—from a colossal squid some 46 feet (14 m) long to pieces of reindeer, horses, and polar bears.

Icy seas *Giant sleeper sharks are the only sharks that survive long-term in polar seas, where the surface can be an icy 28°F (−2°C). Like other large cold-blooded species, they are sluggish and probably use stealth instead of speed to hunt live prey.*

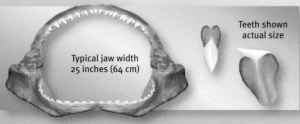

Teeth shown actual size

Typical jaw width 25 inches (64 cm)

Sleepers up close

A sleeper shark's jaws can be about 25 inches (64 cm) across—gaping almost as wide as a great white's. Shaped like curved, smooth spear points, its upper teeth are ideal tools for impaling prey. The lower teeth interlock, forming a blade that can cut through flesh like a kitchen knife.

10-year-old boy 4.5 ft (1.4 m)

Average female Greenland sleeper shark 14 ft (4.3 m)

Cold prey *A peek into the stomach of a Greenland sleeper shark shows that its cold-water prey include fish such as arctic cod. The shark spears the fish with its pointy upper teeth.*

Ups and downs

Greenland sleeper sharks hunt prey such as seals at the surface in winter, but in summer they migrate down to the cooler depths. Cruising in the dark near the seafloor, the sharks hunt octopus and other bottom-dwelling prey but also act like seagoing vultures—scavengers that consume any dead animals they come across.

Sharing the ... More than 20... shark are ada... in the ocean d... sleeper sharks, many have soft bodies and eyes built to detect dim light.

50 ▲ In Foc... Sea ...vel

Hunting blind *Tiny, glowing copepods sometimes attach to the eyeballs of a sleeper shark. The shark becomes blind and must rely on its other senses to locate food. The glowing parasite may help the sleeper by luring prey close to its mouth.*

Bramble shark Covered with blotchy spots and thorns, this rare deep-sea shark is a surprise find near the bottom.

Dark depths *Sleeper sharks dive to inky depths to find the cold water they prefer. Their small eyes are highly sensitive to dim light, including the eerie glow produced by some deep-sea animals.*

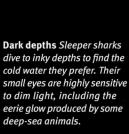

Frilled shark Swimming with their jagged teeth exposed, frilled sharks live on the cold, dark continental slope.

Spiny pygmy shark Light-producing organs on the belly of this tiny, spined shark may help attract mates or confuse potential predators.

False catshark A false catshark eats fish but may also use its wide mouth to scavenge deep-sea garbage. A scientist once found a soda can in a catshark's stomach.

Black dogfish Small cousins of sleeper sharks, black dogfish form schools and migrate up into shallower water in winter.

BULL SHARK: THE FACTS

SPECIES: *Carcharhinus leucas*

GROUP: Requiem sharks (order Carcharhiniformes)

DIET: Fish, including other sharks; marine mammals; sea turtles. Has attacked humans

HABITAT: Tropical coasts and estuaries; sometimes found in freshwater rivers

REPRODUCTION: Live-bearer with litters of about 10 pups; embryos nourished via placenta; gestation 11 months

CONSERVATION STATUS: Near Threatened

SUNLIGHT ZONE

500 ft (150 m)

660 ft (200 m)

TWILIGHT ZONE

3,300 ft (1,000 m)

Bull Shark

Tropical Threat

A fearsome superpredator, the bull shark is the culprit in many serious shark attacks on humans. It hunts prey large and small as it travels through warm coastal waters and estuaries. Most sharks will die if they swim into freshwater, but not the bull shark. With unusual adaptations for managing water and salt in its body, this species can leave the sea and swim upstream a river. Bull sharks regularly turn up in rivers and even lakes in South America, Africa, and India. In the United States they have journeyed more than 1,800 miles (2,900 km) up the Mississippi River to Illinois, while further south in Peru, they have made it 2,300 miles (3,700 km) up the mighty Amazon River.

Treacherous crossing

Hundreds of miles from the sea, a bull shark ambushes a wildebeest crossing a murky river. Bull sharks are aggressive and hefty, usually growing to about 9 feet (2.7 m), and are not afraid to take on big prey. A bull shark may even body-slam a pleasure boat that comes too close.

Dorsal fin *A tall first dorsal fin slicing through the water's surface may be the only clue that an attack is imminent.*

Burly body *The body of a bull shark is broad, stout, and robust. An adult can weigh from 200 to 500 pounds (90–225 kg), with a length ranging from 7 to 11.5 feet (2.1–3.5 m).*

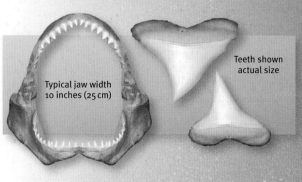

Teeth shown actual size

Typical jaw width 10 inches (25 cm)

Bull sharks up close

Bull sharks have very powerful jaws. The big triangular upper teeth are serrated like a bread knife, making them ideal tools for slicing through large prey such as dolphins, sea turtles, and even other sharks.

10-year-old boy 4.5 ft (1.4 m)

Average female bull shark 9 ft (2.7 m)

Fellow travelers *Zebras follow along with the wildebeest herds. If they make it to the other side of the river, they must then avoid hungry lions waiting in the bush.*

Wildebeest *On their migration across the plains of Africa, vast herds of wildebeest attempt dangerous river crossings. In the water many fall prey to crocodiles and the occasional bull shark.*

Eyes *The bull shark has small eyes and often feeds in murky waters. It relies on other senses for its hunting success.*

Snout *A short, blunt snout inspired the bull shark's common name.*

Pectoral fins *As a bull shark swims, a pair of stiff, pointed pectoral fins provide lift for its heavy, bulky body.*

RIVER SHARKS

Mystery surrounds river sharks such as the Ganges shark. Like bull sharks, they can survive for long periods in rivers and estuaries. Several different species are found in places such as Pakistan, India, and northern Australia, but all are exceedingly rare and probably endangered.

Small, dark eyes

Broad dorsal fin

Sea level

SUNLIGHT ZONE

660 ft (200 m)

900 ft (275 m)

TWILIGHT ZONE

3,300 ft (1,000 m)

☐ Scalloped hammerhead

HAMMERHEADS: THE FACTS

SPECIES: 9 species, all in the family Sphyrnidae

GROUP: Ground sharks (order Carcharhiniformes)

DIET: Fish, squid, octopuses, rays, crustaceans

HABITAT: Warm coastal waters

REPRODUCTION: Live-bearer with litters of 20–50 pups; embryos nourished via placenta; gestation 10 months

CONSERVATION STATUS: Great hammerhead Endangered; golden hammerhead Vulnerable; scalloped, smooth, winghead, and scalloped bonnethead Near Threatened

Gathering together

Scalloped hammerheads often swim in schools made up of hundreds of individuals. Every year in the eastern Pacific Ocean, schools of scalloped hammerheads visit seamounts—undersea peaks where the sharks find plenty of prey.

Hammerheads
A Wide World

Hammerheads are the easiest sharks to identify, thanks to their bizarre hammer-shaped head. Known as a cephalofoil, the head features an eye at either end, a pair of widely separated nostrils on its front edge, and a collection of electricity-sensing organs—all of which help the shark scout for fish, squid, and other prey. Hammerheads swim in warm and tropical seas around the globe. They range from small sharks called bonnetheads and scoopheads, to large smooth hammerheads and scalloped hammerheads. The largest of all is the massive great hammerhead, which can grow as long as 20 feet (6 m) and weigh more than 1,000 pounds (450 kg).

Nostril *A hammerhead follows a scent trail by swimming from side to side, always turning toward the nostril in which the scent is strongest.*

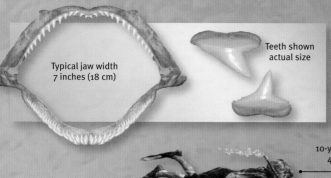

Typical jaw width 7 inches (18 cm)

Teeth shown actual size

Hammerheads up close

Hammerheads have a small mouth and small teeth. The upper teeth of a scalloped hammerhead (left) are notched and bladelike, while the lower teeth are spiky. The comparison below shows small, medium, and large hammerhead species.

10-year-old boy 4.5 ft (1.4 m)

Average female bonnethead shark 3.5 ft (1.1 m)

Average female great hammerhead 12 ft (3.7 m)

Average female scalloped hammerhead 8.5 ft (2.6 m)

Personal space *A dominant hammerhead may use threat displays to prevent other hammerheads from coming too close. Twists, turns, and other gymnastic moves convey the message "Keep your distance."*

School days *In some scalloped hammerhead schools nearly all the sharks are females. The largest females stay in the center of the school, driving away smaller sharks that come too close.*

A winged head *The winglike ends of a hammerhead's cephalofoil allow for greater maneuverability. They work much like airplane wings to lift the front of the shark's body as it swims.*

Eye *Because its eyes are on either side of the "hammer," this shark cannot see directly in front of its snout without turning its head.*

Head shapes
From above, a hammerhead's wide head may look ungainly, but a side view reveals that the head is streamlined, much like the wing of an airplane. The diagrams below show the heads of three hammerhead species from the top and side.

Winghead shark This shark's cephalofoil has the longest and narrowest "wings" of any hammerhead species—they measure roughly half the length of its body. Its nostrils are enormous, each about twice as wide as its mouth. Wingheads live in warm seas between India and Australia.

Smooth hammerhead The lack of a notch in the middle of this large shark's head helps to distinguish it from other hammerheads. The smooth hammerhead occurs worldwide in temperate and tropical zones but prefers cooler water. It is the only hammerhead species found off the coast of Canada.

Bonnethead shark Not all hammerhead species have a winglike head. The bonnethead shark has a more rounded head shaped like a shovel blade, and is sometimes known as the shovelhead. The smallest of the hammerheads, this species lives in warm water off the coasts of both North and South America.

PINNED DOWN

Great hammerheads often feed on other sharks and on rays. The shark uses its head to pin a stingray to the bottom before biting off the ray's wings. Great hammerheads have been found with stingray spines harmlessly stuck in their jaws and stomachs.

Sea level

SUNLIGHT ZONE

660 ft
(200 m)

TWILIGHT ZONE

2,300 ft
(700 m)

3,300 ft
(1,000 m)

WHALE SHARK: THE FACTS

SPECIES: *Rhincodon typus*

GROUP: Carpetsharks (order Orectolobiformes)

DIET: Plankton, crustaceans, squid, small fish

HABITAT: Tropical and warm temperate seas; moves between open ocean and coastal waters; often visible at surface but may dive to more than 2,300 feet (700 m)

REPRODUCTION: Live-bearer with litters of up to 300 pups; embryos nourished by yolk in eggs; gestation unknown

CONSERVATION STATUS: Vulnerable; protected in many places

Whale Shark
Gentle Giant

Giant is the most fitting word for the whale shark, the largest of all the fish in the sea. This immense shark can grow to at least 46 feet (14 m)—longer than a school bus—and weigh up to 15 tons (13.6 t). Despite its massive size, the whale shark is not a fierce, fast-swimming hunter. Instead, like the basking shark and megamouth shark, it is a sluggish filter feeder, with large gills that sieve plankton and other small creatures from seawater. Even more amazing, scientists using satellite tracking discovered that this ocean giant can make vast migrations. One whale shark journeyed from the coast of Mexico to the South Pacific island of Tonga, an incredible trip of more than 8,600 miles (13,800 km).

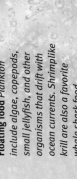

Floating food *Plankton include algae, copepods, small jellyfish, and other organisms that drift with ocean currents. Shrimplike krill are also a favorite whale shark food.*

Open wide *As it feeds, a whale shark moves its head from side to side. The huge mouth may be more than 4 feet (1.2 m) wide.*

Pilot fish *Small pilot fish often travel with whale sharks. They use the shark's massive body like a mobile reef and hide in its shadow.*

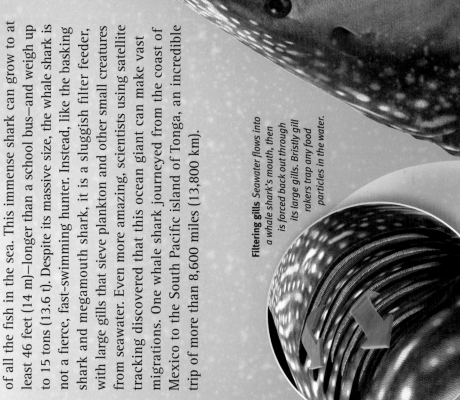

Filtering gills *Seawater flows into a whale shark's mouth, then is forced back out through its large gills. Bristly gill rakers trap any food particles in the water.*

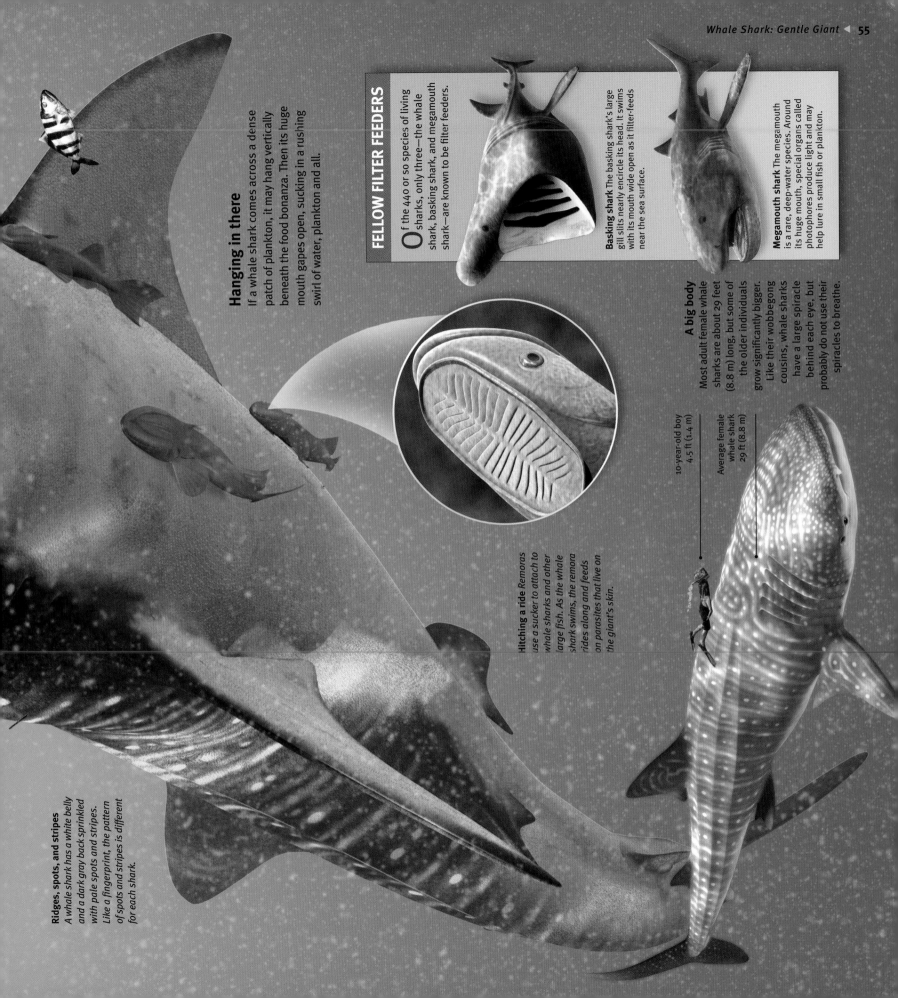

Ridges, spots, and stripes
A whale shark has a white belly and a dark gray back sprinkled with pale spots and stripes. Like a fingerprint, the pattern of spots and stripes is different for each shark.

Hanging in there
If a whale shark comes across a dense patch of plankton, it may hang vertically beneath the food bonanza. Then its huge mouth gapes open, sucking in a rushing swirl of water, plankton and all.

FELLOW FILTER FEEDERS

O f the 440 or so species of living sharks, only three—the whale shark, basking shark, and megamouth shark—are known to be filter feeders.

Basking shark The basking shark's large gill slits nearly encircle its head. It swims with its mouth wide open as it filter-feeds near the sea surface.

Megamouth shark The megamouth is a rare, deep-water species. Around its huge mouth, special organs called photophores produce light and may help lure in small fish or plankton.

Hitching a ride *Remoras use a sucker to attach to whale sharks and other large fish. As the whale shark swims, the remora rides along and feeds on parasites that live on the giant's skin.*

A big body
Most adult female whale sharks are about 29 feet (8.8 m) long, but some of the older individuals grow significantly bigger. Like their wobbegong cousins, whale sharks have a large spiracle behind each eye, but probably do not use their spiracles to breathe.

10-year-old boy
4.5 ft (1.4 m)

Average female
whale shark
29 ft (8.8 m)

Sea level
130 ft (40 m)

SUNLIGHT ZONE

660 ft (200 m)

TWILIGHT ZONE

3,300 ft (1,000 m)

☐ Tasseled wobbegong

WOBBEGONGS: THE FACTS

SPECIES: 8 species, all in the family Orectolobidae

GROUP: Carpetsharks (order Orectolobiformes)

DIET: Bottom-dwelling fish, octopuses, lobsters, crabs

HABITAT: On or near the seafloor in warm temperate and tropical seas, often partly hidden under ledges or rocks

REPRODUCTION: Live-bearer with litters of 20 or more in some species; embryos nourished by yolk in eggs; gestation 6–12 months

CONSERVATION STATUS: Some species Near Threatened

Wobbegongs
On the Bottom

Wobbegongs are the shark world's masters of disguise and surprise. They are wily ambush hunters that live mainly in the warm waters of coral reefs. Lurking on the seafloor or in a coral crevice, a wobbegong looks more like a jumble of spots and dots than a waiting predator. Its large, strong jaws and sharp, scraggly teeth are potent tools for snatching up prey—or for nipping the foot of a careless human who ventures too close. Although wobbegongs certainly rank among the oddest-looking sharks, they are supreme survivors. Scientists believe that wobbegongs have been part of ocean life for more than 160 million years.

Bottom-dweller's tail
A wobbegong's short tail is typical of a bottom-dwelling shark, with two short dorsal fins set far back on the body.

Teeth shown actual size

Typical jaw width 34 inches (85 cm)

Wobbegongs up close
Whether a wobbegong is as short as a young child or as long as a minivan, its jaws have a wide gape for its body size. The gape of a 9.5-foot (2.9-m) ornate wobbegong is 34 inches (85 cm)—nearly one-third of the shark's total body length. Wobbegongs have backward-curving, dagger-sharp teeth to spear their prey.

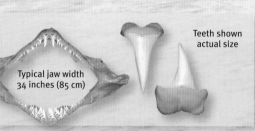

10-year-old boy
4.5 ft (1.4 m)

Average tasselled wobbegong 4 ft (1.2 m)

Average ornate wobbegong 9.5 ft (2.9 m)

Average spotted wobbegong 10.5 ft (3.2 m)

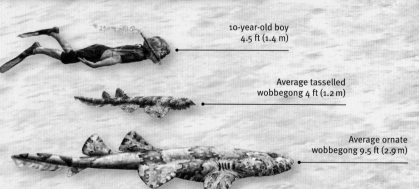

Camouflage *Dark wavy lines and spots blanket a tasseled wobbegong's pale yellow skin. The complex pattern helps camouflage the outlines of the shark's body, making it almost invisible to prey and predators.*

Tempting tassels

The tasseled wobbegong is a mighty mite—only about 4 feet (1.2 m) long. Its name comes from the ragged fringe of skin flaps around its snout and chin. Waving gently in the current, the tassels may seem like tasty morsels to a small fish—luring it close enough to be snapped up.

Ambush attack *Ambush predators stay as still as possible so as not to frighten wary prey. A wobbegong also has lightning reflexes that help it snag a fish the moment one swims by.*

Flattened body *A wobbegong's head and body are flat and wide. The shark will often squeeze under a ledge or lurk in a coral cave, ready to pounce on fish that swim in to hide.*

Large spiracles *Unlike many of the more active sharks, a wobbegong does not have to keep swimming to get the oxygen it needs. Two gaping spiracles allow plenty of water to flow to its gills.*

Decorated snout *The fringe of tassels around the wobbegong's snout attracts small fish. Long barbels on the nostrils help the wobbegong sense its food.*

A SLOW LIFE

If a shark is a bottom-dweller like a wobbegong, chances are that it is fairly small and slowly prowls the seafloor at night. The rest of the time it may tuck into a crevice or cave or hide in a bed of seaweed. Several species can use their pectoral fins to crawl over the bottom.

Chain catshark An elaborate chain pattern marks the skin of this shark (right), which lives on the bottom down to 2,600 feet (800 m) and eats fish, squid, and worms.

Horn shark Only about 2 feet (60 cm) long, horn sharks (left) live in the shallows. They use flat teeth in the rear of their jaws to crush mollusks such as clams.

Sea
level

260 ft
(80 m)

SUNLIGHT ZONE

660 ft
(200 m)

TWILIGHT ZONE

3,300 ft
(1,000 m)

10-year-old boy
4.5 ft (1.4 m)

Average cookiecutter
shark 1.5 ft (45 cm)

COOKIECUTTER SHARK: THE FACTS

ALSO KNOWN AS: Cigar shark

SPECIES: *Isistius brasiliensis*

GROUP: Dogfish sharks (order Squaliformes)

DIET: Bites chunks from large fish and marine mammals;
also feeds on whole octopuses and squid

HABITAT: Deep tropical and warm temperate seas

REPRODUCTION: Live-bearer with litters of 6–12 pups;
embryos nourished by yolk in eggs; gestation unknown

CONSERVATION STATUS: Stable

Cookiecutter Shark
A Sneaky Mouthful

The cookiecutter shark is a voracious hit-and-run artist. Less than 2 feet (60 cm) long, cookiecutters sometimes gulp down squid and octopuses whole, but they specialize in using their razor-sharp teeth to carve cookie-shaped chunks of flesh from large fish, dolphins, seals, and other big prey. They are not afraid to take on huge targets such as whales, and may even inflict bites on passing submarines. Cookiecutters hunt at night near the surface of tropical seas. But with larger predators also on the prowl, they retreat to deep water as dawn approaches, sometimes migrating more than 3,000 feet (900 m) below the waves.

Cigar-shaped body
A cookiecutter shark is shaped like a cigar, with a round, snub-nosed head and a long, slender body. It has a small, paddle-like tail fin.

Teeth at the ready
A cookiecutter's mouth and teeth are at the very front of its stubby snout, at the ready for attaching to prey.

Sub attack
The rubber sonar domes of submarines seem to attract cookiecutter sharks. So do undersea cables, which emit an electric field the sharks can sense. Both may end up pocked with circular bite marks.

Come and get me

Nightfall is the signal for cookiecutters to swim up toward the surface zone to feed. Thanks to light-producing organs called photophores, a cookiecutter's belly glows an eerie green. A dolphin or other large creature may mistake the glow for a catchable fish and swim toward the hungry cookiecutter.

Bioluminescent belly *A network of tiny photophores cover the cookiecutter's belly and produce a greenish light. When a cookiecutter shark dies, its belly continues to glow for a few hours.*

Oily liver *Beneath the cookiecutter's glowing belly is an enormous liver that can make up one-third of its body weight. Brimming with the oil squalene, this liver makes the shark more buoyant.*

Dark collar *A dark band behind a cookiecutter's head may make the shark's glowing belly stand out and the front of its body harder to see.*

Suction cup lips *When a cookiecutter's flexible lips are cupped against a dolphin or other prey animal, the shark's mouth creates strong suction that helps it latch on and scoop out a mouthful of blubber or flesh.*

Large eyes *Wide oval eyes may help the cookiecutter see potential prey in the dimly lit waters where it hunts.*

Small wound *The crater left by a cookiecutter's bite is not serious enough to kill this dolphin. Only about 1 inch (2.5 cm) deep, the wound probably will heal quickly.*

Good enough to eat *A cookiecutter shark sheds an entire band of teeth, then swallows them all. The teeth contain calcium and may help replenish the shark's supply of this key mineral.*

Cutting out a cookie

1. A cookiecutter uses its mouth and upper teeth to attach to a seal. Then its body twists like a doorknob.

2. As the shark swivels, its lower teeth carve out a circle of flesh. The upper teeth hold the plug, and the lower ones scoop it out.

3. After making its quick slice-and-scoop attack, the little shark swims off into the dark ocean to digest its meal.

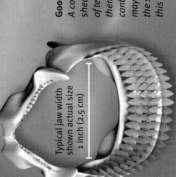

Typical jaw width shown actual size
1 inch (2.5 cm)

The Shark Family Tree

Selachii
All sharks – 9 orders

Pristiophoriformes Sawsharks

Long, sawlike snout with barbels
*9 species including longnose
sawshark, sixgill sawshark*

Longnose sawshark

Hexanchiformes Cowsharks, frilled shark

Single dorsal fin, 6 or 7 gill slits
*5 species including sixgill shark,
sevengill shark, frilled shark*

*Frilled
shark*

*Sevengill
shark*

Squaliformes Dogfish sharks

No saw, not flattened, no thorns on skin
*About 80 species including sleeper sharks,
gulper shark, kitefin, cookiecutter, lanternsharks*

Greenland sleeper

Gulper shark

Echinorhiniformes Bramble sharks

Thorns covering body, pelvic fins
much larger than dorsal fins
*2 species: bramble shark and
prickly shark*

*Bramble
shark*

Squatiniformes Angel sharks

Body flattened with mouth at end of snout
*16 species including Pacific angel shark,
smoothback angel shark*

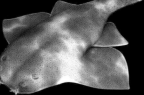

*Pacific
angel shark*

Putting sharks in order

Today's oceans are home to at least 440 species of sharks. All sharks belong to the superorder Selachii, which splits into nine orders. The majority of sharks are ground sharks, members of the order Carcharhiniformes, which includes tiger sharks, hammerheads, and bull sharks.

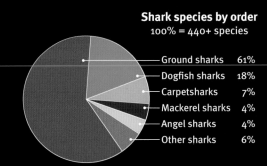

Shark species by order
100% = 440+ species

Ground sharks	61%
Dogfish sharks	18%
Carpetsharks	7%
Mackerel sharks	4%
Angel sharks	4%
Other sharks	6%

Heterodontiformes Bullhead sharks

Dorsal fin spines, sloping forehead, ridges over eyes
9 species including Port Jackson, bullheads, horn sharks

Port Jackson shark

Californian horn shark

Orectolobiformes Carpetsharks

Mouth well in front of eyes, prominent grooves between nostrils and mouth
32 species including whale shark, wobbegongs, nurse shark, zebra shark

Ornate wobbegong

Whale shark

Carcharhiniformes Ground sharks

Nictitating membrane, reproduction variable
270+ species including hammerheads, tiger shark, bull shark, leopard shark, houndsharks, lemon shark, bronze whaler, silky shark, oceanic whitetip, reef sharks, catsharks

Blacktip reef shark

Tiger shark

Great hammerhead

Chain catshark

Lamniformes Mackerel sharks

No nictitating membrane, reproduction viviparous (embryos eat extra eggs)
17 species including great white, makos, threshers, salmon shark, porbeagle, goblin shark, sand tiger, megamouth, basking shark

Great white shark

Bigeye thresher

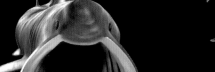

Basking shark

Glossary

ambush predator Carnivore that attacks from a hiding place, using stealth to capture prey.

ampullae of Lorenzini Sensory organs in a shark's head that detect electric fields and help the shark locate potential prey.

anal fin A small fin located in front of the tail on the underside of a fish.

batoid A flat-bodied fish with a cartilage skeleton, such as a ray, skate, guitarfish, or sawfish. A batoid's pectoral fins are attached to the head, and its gill openings are under the head.

bioluminescence The production of light by living creatures. The light may be produced by special organs called photophores, as on the cookiecutter shark, or by bacteria living in the skin, as in some dogfish sharks.

bony fish A fish that has a skeleton made of bone (rather than cartilage).

bottom-dweller A fish or other organism that lives on or near the seafloor.

buoyancy The ability to stay afloat. Oil in a shark's liver provides buoyancy for its body.

bycatch Fish or other animals that are caught in a fishing operation but are not the target species.

camouflage Body colors, patterns, or shapes that help an animal blend in with its surroundings.

carpetshark A shark species that belongs to the order Orectolobiformes. Carpetsharks tend to be small with somewhat flattened bodies, but they include the sea's biggest fish, the whale shark. Most live in tropical parts of the Pacific Ocean.

cartilage Strong, rubbery tissue that forms the skeleton of sharks, batoids, and chimaeras.

cephalofoil The winglike form of a hammerhead shark's head, which extends out on either side.

chimaera Any of the close relatives of sharks known as ratfish, ghost sharks, and elephantfish.

cladodont An extinct group of sharks whose teeth branched into several cusps, each with a cavity containing pulp. Cladodonts were primitive ancestors of modern sharks.

clasper An extension of a male shark's pelvic fin that delivers sperm to the female during mating.

cloaca A chamber in an animal's body that opens to the outside and connects internally to both the reproductive tract and intestine.

continental shelf The shallow, gently sloping submerged edge of a continent.

continental slope The steep slope that begins at the far edge of the continental shelf.

copepod A tiny shrimplike animal. Copepods make up much of the ocean's zooplankton.

countercurrent flow The movement of two fluids in opposite directions. In gills, blood flows through the vessels in the opposite direction of the seawater moving across the gill filaments. Countercurrent flow increases the amount of oxygen a shark's gills extract from the water.

cranium The skull-like cartilage structure that houses a shark's brain.

crustacean An animal such as a shrimp, crab, lobster, or barnacle that has an outer skeleton, antennae, and jointed legs.

dermal denticles Microscopic scales that resemble tiny teeth. Shark skin is covered with dermal denticles.

disk The flattened and rounded main body of a ray or skate.

dogfish shark A shark belonging to the order Squaliformes, which includes spiny dogfish and sleeper sharks. Dogfish sharks do not have anal fins and often have spines on their dorsal fins.

dorsal fin A fin on the back of a fish's body. Most sharks have two dorsal fins.

drag Friction or turbulence that slows down a moving object, such as a swimming shark.

electrosensory organ An organ that detects the presence of electric fields.

embryo An unborn animal in the early stages of development, when its organs and other body parts are not well formed.

estuary A coastal bay where freshwater from a river mingles with seawater.

evolution The changing of animals and plants into different species over millions of years.

extinction The dying out of a species. A mass extinction is when large communities of animals and plants die out at the same time.

fetus An unborn animal in an advanced stage of development. A fetus has all the organs and other body parts of its species.

filter feeder An animal that obtains food by straining small prey from seawater.

finning The practice of cutting off the fins of a living shark and then throwing the shark back in the sea. Many countries have outlawed finning.

fossil The hardened remains of an animal or plant that died many thousands of years ago.

gape The opening created by a shark's jaws.

gestation The period an embryo spends in the mother's uterus until it is ready to be born.

gill arch The skeletal structure that supports a shark's gills.

gill raker In filter-feeding sharks such as whale sharks, a hard structure projecting from a gill arch that filters zooplankton, small fish, and other solids from the water.

gill slits The external openings of a shark's gills.

gills Organs that allow fish to breathe by extracting oxygen from water. Gills are made up of

fine, feather-like structures called filaments.

ground shark A shark belonging to the order Carcharhiniformes, which includes bull sharks, tiger sharks, and hammerheads.

hydrodynamic Designed to move efficiently through the water.

invertebrate An animal without a backbone. Marine invertebrates include worms, shrimps, clams, and octopuses.

krill Tiny shrimplike animals that occur in vast quantities in the ocean. Krill are a key food source for whale sharks and other large filter feeders.

lift Upward force provided by a swimming shark's pectoral fins and tail.

ligament A strap of connective tissue that links one part of the skeleton to another.

live-bearer A species in which the young are born alive after developing inside the mother.

mackerel shark A shark belonging to the order Lamniformes. Examples include salmon sharks, makos, and great white sharks.

mangrove A tree or shrub that grows in swamps and estuaries with its roots mostly underwater.

migration The movement of an animal from one place to another and then back again, often with changing seasons. Most migrations are related to breeding or finding food.

mollusk An aquatic invertebrate such as a clam or squid. Most mollusks have a hard outer shell.

nictitating membrane A thin membrane that can close over an open eye, protecting the eye from damage or debris.

nursery ground A sheltered area, often near shore, where young sharks spend their early life.

pectoral fins A pair of fins located on the side of the body behind the head.

pelvic fins A pair of fins located on the underside of the body, on each side of the cloaca.

photophore A small organ that emits light. In sharks, photophores are in the skin.

phytoplankton Tiny floating plantlike species at or just below the sea's surface. Phytoplankton use sunlight to make their own food via photosynthesis and are the foundation of marine food webs.

placenta A special tissue that connects a growing embryo with the mother's bloodstream during pregnancy.

plankton The community of organisms that float through the sea, rather than actively swimming. Planktonic animals such as copepods and jellyfish are called zooplankton. Plantlike plankton are called phytoplankton.

polar seas Areas of the world ocean around the North or South Poles where the temperature of surface water is at or near freezing.

predator An animal that hunts or preys on other animals for its food.

prey Animals that predators catch to eat.

protrusible Capable of being thrust forward quickly, like the protrusible jaws of sharks.

remora A small fish that uses a special suction disk under its head to attach to another, larger fish. As the remora is carried along, it picks up bits of food left over by its host.

requiem shark A shark belonging to the family Carcharhinidae, a group of ground sharks that includes tiger and bull sharks.

rete mirabile A dense network of small blood vessels. The name means "wonderful net" in Latin.

scavenger An animal that eats the dead remains of other creatures, often parts left by a predator.

semicircular canal A structure in the ear that detects the body's rotation and acceleration.

serrated teeth Teeth with a jagged, sawlike edge, which can cut through thick flesh.

species One kind of organism, such as a great white shark, an ornate wobbegong, or a human being. Members of the same species have the same general body form and functions and rarely or never produce offspring with other species.

spiracle An opening behind the eyes of rays and some of the less active sharks. Depending on the species, spiracles pump water to the gills or carry it to special blood vessels that pick up oxygen while the animal is resting.

spiral valve A section of a shark's small intestine that contains folds twisted like a spiral staircase. The spiral valve increases the surface area that can absorb nutrients from food.

squalene An oil in the liver of a deep-sea shark that increases the shark's buoyancy.

superpredator A large predator that may prey on many other animals but has few or no natural enemies of its own.

tapetum lucidum A layer of cells behind or inside the back of the eye that reflects light into the retina and makes it sensitive to low light.

temperate seas Areas of the world ocean between the tropical and polar regions where surface water averages about 50°F (10°C).

tropical seas Areas of the world ocean on either side of the Equator, where surface water averages above 69°F (20°C).

uterus A baglike organ where young develop. Female sharks have two uteri.

vertebrae Hard segments that make up the spinal column of a vertebrate.

vertebrate An animal with a backbone.

zooplankton Aquatic animals that float with currents. Most zooplankton are extremely small.

Index

Credits

The publisher thanks Alexandra Cooper for her contribution, and Puddingburn for the index.

Key t=top; l=left; r=right; tl=top left; tcl=top center left; tc=top center; tcr=top center right; tr=top right; cl=center left; c=center; cr=center right; b=bottom; bl=bottom left; bcl=bottom center left; bc=bottom center; bcr=bottom center right; br=bottom right

ILLUSTRATIONS
Front cover The Art Agency (Mick Posen main, cr; Barry Croucher tr, br)
Back cover The Art Agency (Barry Croucher tr; Thomas Bayley l, b)
Spine The Art Agency (Mick Posen)
The Art Agency (Thomas Bayley) 12t, 14-15bl, cl, c, br, tr, 16-17l, 34-5l, b, 46l, 50-1l, r, 52-3l, r, 54-5t, l, br, 56-7l, br, 58-9br; **(Robin Carter)** 20-1b; **(Barry Croucher)** 8l, 18-19, 20-1, 22-3, 26-7, 30, 32-3, 48-9, 50-1, 54-5, 56-7; **(Rob Davis)** 8b, r, 22l, 24l, 36-7t, b, 40l; **(Gary Hanna)** 22tl, br, 34-5, 36, 40-1, 50-1; **(Terry Pastor)** 10-11, 12-13, 18-19, 28-9, 39tr; **(Mick Posen)** 14-15,

16-17, 18l, 22r, 24-5, 29br, 38-9, 42-3, 46-7, 52-3, 58-9; **(Jurgen Ziewe)** 11b & size boy; **Christer Eriksson** 8-9
MAPS
Andrew Davies; Map Illustrations

PHOTOGRAPHS
AAP = Australian Associated Press; CBT = Corbis; GI = Getty Images; PL = photolibrary.com; SP=Seapics.com
10tcr GI **20**cl CBT. cl PL **24**tr SP **28**cl SP **30**cl, cr SP **31**bl PL br, c SP tr CBT **38**l AAP **41**br PL **42**bcl PL tr CBT

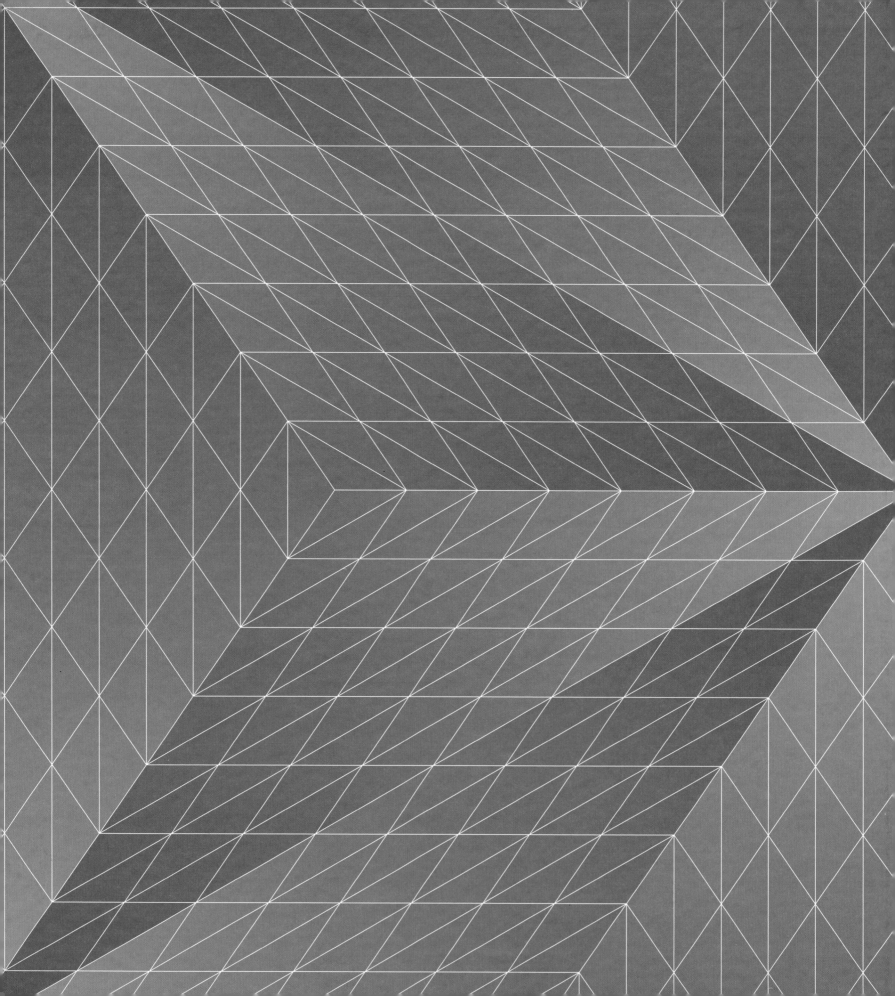